ALCOHOLISM
and Christian Experience

ALCOHOLISM
and Christian Experience

By C. ROY WOODRUFF
Foreword by Wayne E. Oates

THE WESTMINSTER PRESS
PHILADELPHIA

Copyright © MCMLXVIII The Westminster Press

LIBRARY OF CONGRESS CATALOG CARD NO. 68–15438

Published by The Westminster Press®
Philadelphia, Pennsylvania

PRINTED IN THE UNITED STATES OF AMERICA

To KAY
*who has taught
me the meaning
of Christian experience
in the covenant
of marriage*

Foreword

The great traditions of William James and Anton Boisen
in the study of religious experience are brought into new
expression in this study of the aching necessities and hopeful redemption of the alcoholic. Roy Woodruff studies alcoholism empirically through the use of primary documents
of individuals' autobiographies. In this respect he is in the
tradition of William James. He consults " the living human
documents " of the suffering persons themselves rather than
the dusty volumes of a library shelf as his primary sources.
In this he is in the tradition of Anton Boisen. He goes beyond these traditions by relying heavily upon the accumu-
lated research of the Rutgers School of Alcohol Studies and
empirical studies done by others.

Yet the uniqueness of Roy Woodruff himself as a Christian pastor shows through these pages. I am personally ac-
quainted with some of the alcoholics with whom Woodruff
worked as he developed the study that you are about to
read. He did not " treat " these persons as " cases." He related to them as persons. He built durable relationships of
concern and commitment to them as he worked on the
points of view expressed in these pages. This, therefore,
is a remarkable demonstration that research can be something more than, other than, and different from a dissec-

tion of persons as if they were things and not human beings. Christian commitment to persons in distress does not rule out the factual concern and the respect for empirical methodology inherent in the scientific method. The research done by a Christian pastor, therefore, is unique — or at least should be — in this respect. Woodruff's work sets a pattern of research that can be assimilated into the practice of the Christian ministry and therefore should be a challenge to more working pastors to focus a research concern upon their service to persons.

Again, the attempt to shrug when the phrase " Christian conversion " is mentioned in connection with the plight of the alcoholic is both avoided and challenged by Woodruff in this book. He takes Christian conversion seriously without being naïve. He looks at its results with neither jaundiced nor moonstruck eyes. He looks at a conversion experience as it is and in terms of the long-term results of it in relation to the life pattern of the alcoholic. In doing so, he both strengthens our confidence in the power of the gospel in relation to the alcoholic and underscores the ambiguities and contingencies in this therapy of redemption. Christian conversion as therapy hazards all the ambiguities and contingencies hazarded by any other form of therapy.

Underneath all these results is the quiet communication and clear directive of an author experienced in dealing directly with alcoholics; i.e., no *one* therapy is the imperial therapy of choice for the alcoholic. The community that the alcoholic desperately needs must begin also in the community of the different therapies for alcoholism. Combined forces of the whole community are necessary. The church as community, often accused of dividing the community, is called upon to be the catalyst to bring together the healing forces of the whole community. The stresses and strains behind the desperation of the alcoholic and his family dramatically spell the suffering of the whole community in large print. The more we learn about the ministry of the church to the alcoholic, the more likely we are to find clues to the very nature of the church itself. The resolution of other problems that beset the people within and without the church becomes more evident. Roy Woodruff, a hard-working Christian pastor and a skilled researcher and writer, gives you such guidance in this disciplined volume.

WAYNE E. OATES

Louisville, Kentucky

Acknowledgments

The talents and interests of many persons have gone into the writing of this book. I am deeply indebted to each person who has contributed to it. My gratitude is extended to Professors Wayne E. Oates, Samuel Southard, Penrose St. Amant, and John W. Carlton, who guided me through the original research and writing of this manuscript in the Graduate School of the Southern Baptist Theological Seminary. Especial thanks must be given to Dr. Oates, who not only gave wise and sensitive guidance in the early stages of writing but who also provided me with constant support and encouragement, freely offered in the context of a warm, faithful friendship. My debt to him cannot be repaid, but the joy is that repayment is not a demand in an open, committed relationship. The paper that is the real genesis of this study is found as Chapter VII in Dr. Oates's book, *Alcohol: In and Out of the Church* (Broadman Press, 1966). It was a joint effort between Dr. Oates and myself. I am also grateful to him for the Foreword included in this book.

A research grant was provided by the Division of Alcohol Problems and General Welfare, Board of Christian Social Concerns of The Methodist Church, to support expenses incurred in the process of this study. This grant relieved financial pressure during the months of intensive research and writing and was of great benefit to myself and to the completion of the study.

Deep appreciation is felt toward the recovered alcoholics who participated so willingly in this study. Without their help, this book could never have been written. I will not forget the friendships that were established in the months during which the research took place. I found myself being ministered unto through the witness given to the grace of God in the lives of these people. Their genuineness and openness served as living illustrations of the capacity of the human personality for change and renewal.

Others who gave able assistance to this project were Dr. Ronald Lindner, clinical psychologist, the Reverend Roscoe Tarter, a friend and counselor of alcoholics, Dr. Ronald Deering, research librarian, and Mrs. Barbara McJenkins, who worked faithfully in typing the final copy of the manuscript. These are just a few of the many who have participated in the process of this study.

One other person made the completion of this book possible — my wife. As a constant source of encouragement and help, she gave up many, many hours to read the manuscript, make wise editorial suggestions, and type the rough draft. Her love and support has never meant more than during the months of work represented by this book. It is to her that this book is dedicated.

C. R. W.

Contents

Contents

CHAPTER I

Introduction

ALCOHOLISM is both a crisis and a chronic situation in which the dynamics of human needs and behavior rise to the surface and are acted out in many ways. These needs have been in the individual all the time. Alcoholism is a catalytic experience that brings the individual into open and direct confrontation with his needs. He can no longer repress them from his consciousness and maintain his self-sufficiency. He can no longer hide his inadequacies from others. He becomes the puppet rather than the puppeteer. His only hope is in severing the alcoholic strings that control him and in becoming motivated from within.

This drama takes place in the theater of life. The actor is a real person, speaking his own dialogue, and portraying the struggle of his own existence. As a drama, alcoholism has an audience. All who come in contact with the alcoholic can see what is happening. They may not understand, but, nevertheless, they see. It is a dangerous drama in that the closer a person is to the life-and-death struggle taking place " onstage," the more likely he is to be hurt himself.[1]

The conflictual nature of human personality, with its struggle to find self, its need for redemption, and its mysterious relationship with its creator, is dramatically portrayed in the experience of the alcoholic. Seldon D. Bacon notes that a study of alcoholism provides "a remarkable vantage point for the study of man and society." [2] Although this book does not claim to be more than a study of the problem of Christian experience in the process of alcoholism, the hope is that the reader will see the wider implications this study can have for an approach to alcoholism, and an understanding of human nature with its struggle for wholeness and meaning. This book focuses on the Christian conversion of the alcoholic and the nature of his relationship to a given Protestant church. It attempts to encompass neither the whole field of alcoholism nor all the broad dimensions of conversion.

The study began with questions that have not been answered previously. The author wanted to know what Christian experience means to an alcoholic. What are the dynamics of his conversion experience? What is the role of the church in the life of the alcoholic? The most reliable source for the answers is the alcoholic himself.

Francis W. McPeek writes, " It is faith in the living God which has accounted for more recoveries from the disease [alcoholism] than all the other therapeutic agencies put together." [3] While this is a provoking statement, it is related to no clinical evidence. The meaning of this " faith in the living God " is not explored. Even though Howard J. Clinebell, Jr., has given significant help toward an understanding of the religious experience in alcoholism by saying that " religion has genuine answers to the spiritual problems to which alcohol gives pseudoanswers," there is a lack of investigation into the dynamic realities of religious experience.[4] This illustrates the present void in empirical research into the role of Christian experience in alcoholism.

This book attempts to explore various manifestations of Christian experience in the lives of a group of alcoholics. The second chapter points out different meanings of conversion in the human experience of alcoholism. However, unless it is otherwise designated, any reference to conversion in this book will mean specifically Christian conversion.

Frank Stagg, a professor of New Testament interpretation, defines conversion as the experience in which

> one is brought into the way of God, which is the way of the cross. Man is delivered from the Adamic way of self-love, self-trust, self-assertion, self-worship to the way of the cross, the way of self-denial and self-giving rooted in faith in God.[5]

William James indicates that in conversion there is a shift in the " habitual center of . . . personal energy," a transition of one's own life force in a new channel.[6]

This directional shift, which is the hallmark of conversion, is also noted by Charles Stinnette, who says that

> Christian experience has signalized in repentance and conversion the crucial moment for turning away from the rigidly striving self to a relaxed trust in God. . . . Conversion is a returning movement of the creature to the Creator.[7]

Edgar Y. Mullins spoke of the essence of conversion as a changed will.[8] Conversion takes place through a decision of the will. This decision is possible only through the grace of God. " A converted man is one in whom the grace of God has wrought a spiritual change." [9] Mullins stresses the centrality of Christ in the conversion. " Conversion is the word employed in theology to designate the turning of a sinner from his sins unto Christ for his salvation." [10]

As one can see from these sources, the main thrust of Christian conversion is understood to be the positive change of direction that occurs within the life of an individual. From self-destruction, he moves to salvation through the grace of God. A growing consciousness of Christ is essential in this experience. However, one's Christ-consciousness may be very dim and hazy in the initial stages of conversion. Conversion is uniquely Christian when, in the maturing process of turning from self to the creating and sustaining

Power outside of self, the individual understands God in terms of the incarnation of Jesus Christ.

Numerous misconceptions surround the term " alcoholism." An authoritative definition of alcoholism is found in *The Alcohol Language: With a Selected Vocabulary,* by Mark Keller and John R. Seeley, as follows:

> A chronic disease, or disorder of behavior, characterized by the repeated drinking of alcoholic beverages to an extent that exceeds customary dietary use or ordinary compliance with the social drinking customs of the community, and that interferes with the drinker's health, interpersonal relations or economic functioning.[11]

The person caught up in this destructive process is an " alcoholic." An oversimplified definition of this descriptive term is: one who is addicted to alcohol. A more adequate, yet easily understandable definition, is given by Alfred Agrin, psychiatric consultant at the Georgia Clinic and Rehabilitation Center for Alcoholics. Dr. Agrin defines an alcoholic in two ways:

> 1. The alcoholic is a person for whom the desire for the intake of alcohol in some form or other becomes stronger, more or less frequently, and more or less regularly than even the most basic of human instincts. These basic human instincts are commonly supposed to be sex, hunger, and self-preservation.
> 2. The alcoholic, to me, is the person who " must " have a drink before he can do the next step in living, whether this step is eating, working, dancing or paying one's bills. This does not mean that the alcoholic, from time to time, does not pay his bills or eat or have sexual and social relations, but it does mean that frequently he needs and " must have " some alcoholic beverage within him in order to feel comfortable in doing so.[12]

The most important point to be stressed in understanding the alcoholic is: the alcoholic is a person, an individual, a creature of God for whom God has given himself. The compulsions of the alcoholic differ from those of the non-alcoholic only in the object of his compulsions and maybe, but not necessarily, in the intensity of his compulsions. Like many persons who suffer from a multitude of ills, both physical and mental, the alcoholic is a sick person. Like all persons, the alcoholic cannot redeem himself. He must surrender to a higher power outside of himself if he is to find himself and be restored to the "land of the living."

The alcoholics studied in this project are those who have a relationship to a Protestant church. The phrase "parish fellowship" is used instead of simply "church" or "local church" to distinguish between the activities of the church and the persons within the church. A person who may or may not be related to the activities of the church is still a part of the parish fellowship. It is this wider fellowship or community that is considered in this study.

This fellowship may be an organized denominational church, or it may be a mission that, in itself, is a continous community. Ideally, it should be "a community of acceptance, humility, and love in which personal faith can grow."[13] However, Samuel Southard is right when he says that "although the church is the agency that is to stimulate spiritual growth, it sometimes erects barriers to the individuality which it should promote."[14] The Protestant parish fellowship, which is the context of this study, may be described as that community of persons who are identified with one another through a common faith in Jesus Christ, who are affiliated with a local, recognized group under the direction of a pastor, and who observe regular services of worship in a specified place. The strengths and weaknesses of the parish fellowship in ministering to the alcoholic are explored in this book.

Actual case material is the primary source for the documentation of the study. The cases were obtained through depth interviews with the alcoholics. Each person who was interviewed gave permission for his case to be used by the author. The anonymity of the respondents is respected and actual names are not used. The sampling consisted of twenty persons who have experienced alcoholism, who have given evidence of Christian experience, and who are, in some degree, related to a local Protestant parish. The sampling represented a wide sociocultural cross section and a variety of denominational affiliations. It included alcoholics who are related to Alcoholics Anonymous and those who are not. The alcoholics may or may not have successfully maintained sobriety, although the majority of those interviewed have remained sober. Each person in the sampling had been sober for the period of at least one year previous to the interview. The various durations of sobriety ranged from one year to twenty years, most of them being under eight years. The ages represented in the sampling ranged from age thirty-nine to sixty-two, a span of twenty-three years, which is the period of mature adulthood. Both men and women were interviewed. The alcoholics knew that the interviewer was a minister. They responded with enthusiasm and appreciated the interest expressed in the religious dimension of their experience. The clinical research was seen from the perspective of pastoral care, and the persons in the sampling were treated with concern and respect. Several said that the interview had given them new insight. Warm and meaningful friendships were formed during the clinical research.

Since this is a qualitative rather than a numerical study, the data are interpreted in terms of meanings and dynamics rather than statistics and percentages. It is felt that a qualitative study is the best way to explore and interpret human personality and experience at a depth level. The authorities on Christian conversion in alcoholism are not scholars and writers. They are the persons who have been " to hell and back " in alcoholism, and who know what conversion means to them as despairing selves. With the clinical material as a basis, theological and psychological sources are used as means of insight into and understanding of the dynamics of human experience. Both clinical data and theoretical formulations mean relatively little when each stands alone. However, when the two are brought together, they become effective means of discovery and interpretation.

To gain a clear understanding of the experience of Christian conversion, reference must be made to sources in the discipline of theology. Much of what has been written on conversion is repetitive and lacks originality of thought. For that reason, primary sources from the writings of influential American theologians and religious leaders are sought as the theological authorities for this study. The material of Jonathan Edwards, Edgar Y. Mullins, Reinhold Niebuhr, and Daniel Day Williams is among that utilized. Added to these sources are the writings of those men who have attempted to bridge the gap between theology and psychology while maintaining their foothold in theology. These are men such as Anton Boisen, Wayne E. Oates, David E. Roberts, Seward Hiltner, Samuel Southard, and others.

The study of conversion came early in the history of psychology of religion in America. In 1891, G. Stanley Hall wrote on religious conversion in adolescence, maintaining that conversion was simply an expected reaction of adolescent experience. Following Hall's lead, other men began a study of conversion, using questionnaires, interviews, and other accepted methods of psychological research. Perhaps the most constructive work was that done by William James in 1902. His *The Varieties of Religious Experience* has remained a classic in the psychological understanding of religious experience. Edwin D. Starbuck, George A. Coe, James B. Pratt, Elmer T. Clark, Henry N. Wieman and his wife, Regina Westcott-Wieman, were among those who made significant contributions to the psychology of religious conversion in the first third of this century.

Although these early sources are significant, they are somewhat outdated by more contemporary theories of personality. A holistic approach has more to say about the total meaning of human experience. The basic psychological sources, therefore, are drawn from current works in psychology. The journal articles of Harry M. Tiebout and Leon Salzman are relevant to this as well as the writings of Erik Erikson. One chapter is given to an examination of the clinical data in the light of the theories of András Angyal and Kazimierz Dabrowski. The writings of these men lend fresh insight into the experience of alcoholism.

CHAPTER II

Categories of Conversion
in Alcoholism

WILLIAM JAMES defined conversion as

> the process, gradual or sudden, by which a self hither-
> to divided, and consciously wrong, inferior, and un-
> happy, becomes unified and consciously right, su-
> perior, and happy, in consequence of its firmer hold
> upon religious realities.[1]

The individual undergoes a shift in his life direction. In the
experience of total conversion, " religious ideas, previously
peripheral in his consciousness, now take a central place,
and . . . religious aims form the habitual centre of his
energy." [2] Psychology, says James, cannot explain the *how*
and *why* of this shift. It can only describe what has happened. Rather than establishing a norm for all experiences,
James places emphasis on the individual experience. With
this approach to human experience, James is more relevant
than he is sometimes given credit for. This study, although
differing at points, supports the fundamental validity of
James's conception of conversion.

James's definition has been challenged, however, by
Earl H. Furgeson, of Wesley Theological Seminary.[3] Fur-
geson maintains that James is erroneous at three points.
The first error is in stating that conversion is " gradual or

sudden." Furgeson says that conversion is a sudden event
that is restricted to a narrowly defined crisis experience. It
is not gradual. Secondly, Furgeson suggests an error in the
assumption that sudden conversion is an experience that is
related to the process of growth. He sees it as being radically
different from the process of growth. His third criticism is
that it is not reliable to assume that " the event of conversion is always regenerative and progressive." [4] He sees conversion as an event that may be either regressive or progressive.

Furgeson's attack on James places him in conflict with
Walter Houston Clark, of Andover Newton Theological
School, who gives full support to James's definition. [5] Clark
states that many modern psychologists do not take James
very seriously for two reasons: they consider him out of
date, and they believe that " he does not fit neatly into the
modern conception of what psychology should be." [6] Clark
characterizes James as an " expander " rather than a " sys-
tematizer." His expansive mind explored new areas with
vitality and insight. He was less concerned with the careful explanation of causation of phenomena and structur-
ing theories. Therefore, " James' contributions to the psychology of religious conversion were not so much in the
form of established fact or carefully contrived systems of
ideas as they are in the form of attitudes, emphases, and
stimulating insights." [7] He used case material extensively
and he was more concerned to sample the flavor of a living
experience than to reduce it to statistical analysis. He focused on the being of the individual.

The different stances taken by Furgeson and Clark on
James's psychology of conversion illustrate one thing. An
agreement upon the understanding of the conversion experience has not yet taken place. It indicates, as well, that
a study of conversion continues to be a lively topic for research. The new insights of dynamic psychology have added
fresh thoughts on old subjects. Even though different types
of conversion experiences have been described, there is a

need for descriptive categories of conversion. The varieties of conversion in alcoholism fall into categories of experience.

Case histories show that Furgeson and Clark have valid and invalid insights into the psychology of conversion described by William James. These insights will be mentioned in the development of this chapter. There are similarities and differences in the experiences of converted alcoholics that, when viewed holistically, fall into four categories of conversion: psychosocial conversion, restrictive Christian conversion, limited Christian conversion, and comprehensive Christian conversion. The following pages describe and illustrate these categories.

I. PSYCHOSOCIAL CONVERSION

Conversion is not limited to religious concepts. It is a psychological phenomenon that can occur apart from any religious interpretation. Harry M. Tiebout, a psychiatrist and a past president of the National Committee on Alcoholism, has made valuable contributions to understanding the psychological conversion of an alcoholic. He defines conversion as " a psychological event in which there is a major shift in personality manifestation." [8] One set of feelings disappears and a radically different set emerges. The individual shifts from a negative to a positive state of mind. This change has " many of the earmarks of religious conversion," but it has no religious basis.[9] Tiebout describes one of his patients as having experienced a shift in personality manifestation through contact with Alcoholics Anonymous. The patient's " aggression subsided materially, her feeling of being at odds with the world disappeared, and with it vanished her tendency to suspect the motives and attitudes of others." [10] The " hard inner core " of her personality was removed and she was at peace with her world.

This category is *psychosocial conversion.* The individual

is transformed both in his self-concept and in his relationship to others. The psychosocial conversion remains on a psychological and social level. It is a horizontal, as opposed to a vertical, experience. There is a sense of release and a new direction in life, but no conception of transcendent powers intervening in one's life. Tiebout says that this kind of conversion is "not consciously willed, but arising from changes in the unconscious psychodynamics," which cause a shift of inner feelings.[11]

The Case of Mr. Mallory. Psychosocial conversion can be illustrated in the life of Mr. Mallory, an upper-middle-class executive. This middle-aged man had an adequate, steady income, prominent status in the community, an attractive wife, and two children. His father was a nonparticipating Protestant, and his mother was a nominal Catholic. Mr. Mallory stopped attending church when he was about fifteen. He joined a Presbyterian church with his wife when he married, but he attends only once a year. He has very little, if any, concept of God.

Mr. Mallory had been a social drinker for many years before he became an alcoholic. His alcohol addiction began to interfere with his family life and interpersonal relationships. He had a violent temper. He became restless and irresponsible. Quick trips across the country became customary during drinking sprees. He would be gone for days without telling his wife where he was. Driving while intoxicated led to several serious automobile accidents that could easily have killed him, but all of which he survived.

Mr. Mallory made several attempts to stop drinking, but he could not overcome his addiction. Finally, when he felt that he was a hopeless case of alcoholism, he decided that it would be best for everyone if he just left town secretly and walked out of the lives of his family and friends. The irrationality of his alcoholic mind led him to do this, thinking it would solve his family's problem. He flew to another city and checked into a hotel. While alone in his hotel room, Mr. Mallory thought over his situation. The idea came to

him, "Maybe I *can* make it — maybe I *can* stay sober."
With that ray of hope entering his darkness, he flew back
home, entered Alcoholics Anonymous, and has remained
sober for seven years.

From an egocentric, irresponsible way of life, this man
was converted to an open, considerate, and responsible attitude toward himself and others. He is an honest, affable,
and genuine person who relates warmly to those around
him. The psychosocial conversion was "triggered" by his
saying, "Maybe I *can* make it." This small hope was all he
needed to redirect his way of life. His nonreligious outlook
on life is expressed by his saying: "I don't even know if
there is a God or not, but I know that I love people and
everything that lives. I would wreck my car before I would
hit a *dog* in the road!" He says that he cannot even claim
to be an agnostic, because he does not know enough about
God to doubt His existence. However, Mr. Mallory is seeking to find God. He faithfully attended a religious discussion group each week and contributed meaningfully to the
group discussion. His psychosocial conversion may grow
into a Christian conversion in the process of his own maturation.

The State of Assurance. This recovered alcoholic is experiencing what William James calls "the state of assurance," rather than "the faith state." [12] Faith connotes religious belief, which is absent from this man's experience.

The state of assurance contains three characteristics.
"The central one is the loss of all the worry, the sense that
all is ultimately well with one, the peace, the harmony, the
willingness to be, even though the outer conditions should
remain the same." [13] James points out that the Christian
concepts of grace and salvation may be entirely lacking, and
yet the affective peace remains the same. Mr. Mallory gives
evidence of his own sense of assurance by his realistic acceptance of sobriety and his ability to relate to others of all
classes and backgrounds. He does not manifest any anxiety
about his religious inadequacy, even though he sees a need

at that point. He possesses an inner confidence which pervades his social relationships.

"The second feature is the sense of perceiving truths not known before." [14] Mr. Mallory makes perceptive and stimulating comments in religious discussions. He listens carefully to all that is said and reflects intelligently upon it. He has an alert mind and an articulate manner of speaking.

"A third peculiarity of the assurance state is the objective change which the world often appears to undergo." [15] Subjects and objects in the world that were previously meaningless take on a new beauty and depth of value. Mr. Mallory indicates this feeling through his tender attitude toward all living things. He has a deep respect for life, wherever it may be found.

The Case of Mr. Goode. Another case that illustrates psychosocial conversion is that of Mr. Goode, a lower-class worker in late middle age. When Mr. Goode was three years old his father died. He was reared in a strict home and forced to go to Sunday school and church by his mother. As soon as he became old enough to get a job, he stopped attending church and began to drink. He made a good income, but, as his drinking became compulsive, he spent most of it on liquor. He had no contact with the church. At one time his wife threatened to leave him if he did not stop drinking. He refused to stop, she left, and he went on a six-month bender.

He realized he had hit bottom and needed his wife; therefore he submitted to her demands to stop drinking if she would come back to him. She came back and he did not drink for two years. However, he was unhappy during this time because he wanted to drink. His wife " was holding a big stick " over his head, threatening to leave him if he drank again. Finally, he told her she could " go to hell," but he was going to drink. She did not leave, even though he resumed drinking. Mr. Goode knew he was a confirmed alcoholic, but all that mattered to him was getting drunk. He lost all self-respect.

One night Mr. Goode was driven home by one of his drinking buddies. He got out of the car in a drunken stupor. Living next door to the Goodes was a young couple. As Mr. Goode started toward his house, he saw the young wife in front of her house. He turned toward her, approaching her with crude and vulgar language. The young wife's husband heard him and came out of the house. Somehow, without any conflict, they got Mr. Goode home. This was a redemptive act in itself.

The next morning Mr. Goode had absolutely no recollection of the incident, but his wife, the husband of the young woman next door, and several other people who heard him told him what he had said and done. Mr. Goode was struck with a deep sense of shame and regret. He had never done anything like that before. To find out about his shameful conduct was a sudden and painful shock to him. He said: "I'm not that kind of man! If that is what alcohol makes me do, I'll never drink again." That was more than ten years ago. He has not had a drink since then. He says he has no desire to drink, and he knows that if he takes one drink now, the desire will overwhelm him. When asked what it was that caused him to stop drinking and make such a radical transformation, his reply was, " shame."

Mr. Goode has a pleasant, congenial personality and relates quite well to other persons. He talks freely, but not compulsively, about his alcoholism. Apparently, Mr. Goode has radically shifted his personality expression. One of the ways he says he has changed is in his regard for other people. While he was drinking, his only concern was alcohol. He was infantile, self-centered, and cared little for the feelings of others. Now he is no longer egocentric. He gets much pleasure out of helping others. Mr. Goode is not a Christian, but he " tries to do right." He talks of an " emptiness " in his life and his need to become a Christian.

The cases of Mr. Mallory and Mr. Goode give clinical evidence that the conversion phenomenon is not *necessarily* religious.[16] The dynamics of these conversions are similar to the Christian conversion, but awareness of God's grace and redemption in Jesus Christ is absent. Christian conversion can be understood more adequately when one is aware of the dynamics of nonreligious, psychosocial conversion. William Sargant has pointed out that the dynamics and methods of conversion are used and experienced in many places and for many different purposes.[17]

The fact that these two men are asking religious questions indicates that psychosocial conversion is not a complete experience of the total personality, even though a personality shift does take place. It suggests a spiritual dimension of the human personality which also needs conversion. When total conversion is lacking, an emptiness is left in the individual's life that he strives to fill. His spiritual needs may motivate him toward a religious experience.

II. Restrictive Christian Conversion

A second category of conversion in alcoholism has an explicit religious basis. It is a Christian conversion in which the individual experiences a divine-human encounter and organizes his life around the revelation of God in Jesus Christ. However, he is restricted to a legalistic, rigid set of spiritual rules that he must follow if he maintains sobriety. There is a change in his relationships with others, but it is not a total change. He cannot relate to those who do not agree with him. Although he may help some people, he antagonizes others by using his conversion as a norm that he imposes upon all other alcoholics. He becomes a closed self with restricted vision. Wayne E. Oates points out the possibility that the person may burden " himself with the necessity of developing finer and finer distinctions to assure himself of his own perfection and freedom from error." [18] The individual " who pushes his own need to be perfect to the extremes of the unforgiving legalist may also confuse his concept of God with his concept of himself." [19] This person, therefore, becomes the teacher of religious experience and is no longer open to new learning about himself.

This category is *restrictive Christian conversion.* It is similar to what Leon Salzman, a psychiatrist, calls " regressive religious conversion." Salzman sees religious conversion as characteristic of the process of change in human adaptation.

> In the process of fulfilling human needs, some people follow a rather direct course, with minimal strife and turmoil, while others face major obstacles which require major adjustments. These major adjustments may constitute constructive, regressive movements.[20]

The term " restrictive " is preferred over Salzman's term " regressive." Regressive connotes a backward movement from the preconversion state. In the alcoholic's experience, that would be a false connotation. In this conversion experience, research indicated improvement in his way of life after he gave up alcohol. However, he is restricted to the conversion experience itself and does not grow beyond it.

Static Salvation. David E. Roberts calls this experience " static salvation." [21]

> The static view assumes that ethical and religious progress is most effectively promoted, and the perils of indifference and irresponsibility are best avoided, by holding before the eyes of men a vision of perfection which will keep them perpetually ashamed of themselves.[22]

The consequences of static salvation are hypocrisy, self-righteousness, and, possibly, unresolved despair. The individual with a restricted conversion experience projects a false sense of security. He justifies his rigidity with a sense of exalted worth. However, when these patterns break down, he is in danger of pathological depression.

Change of Nature. In describing the spiritual affections that accompany genuine conversion, Jonathan Edwards listed one of the signs of spiritual affections as " a change of nature." [23] By this, Edwards meant a total change. "The change that is wrought in conversion, is a universal change: grace changes a man with respect to whatever is sinful in him." [24] Edwards indicated that a man may forsake other sins but retain his major sin, "the iniquity he is chiefly inclined to." [25] This prohibits a total "change of nature" and restricts the spiritual and personal growth of the individual. András Angyal, a psychiatrist, would call this reaction a "part process," in which a part of the personality disrupts the function of the total personality. [26] Thus, in restrictive Christian conversion, a total "change of nature" cannot take place.

The Sin of Pride. The penetrating insight of Reinhold Niebuhr marks the basis of human sin as pride. There are different forms of pride, but Niebuhr says that one form, "the pride of self-righteousness, rises to a form of spiritual pride, which is . . . not a specific form of pride at all but pride and self-glorification in its inclusive and quintessential form." [27] The sin of pride is generally man's major sin and the one to which he clings when all the rest are disposed of. This prohibits a "change of nature" and designates a restrictive Christian conversion.

Alcoholics cannot live with their pride and self-glorification, but they feel that they would be reduced to nothing without it. It is very easy for "alcoholic pride" to be converted into "spiritual pride" in the process of Christian conversion. This perhaps is the converted alcoholic's greatest temptation. One person said that when he hit bottom as an alcoholic and finally reached the place where he could take an honest personal inventory, he found that alcohol was just one of many problems. His basic problem was pride. Coming out of a deprived background, he had worked hard to achieve status and recognition. He had been extremely successful. As an ambition-ridden self who was in competition with life, he placed himself over others as a superior, self-sufficient being.

This man realized that if he was going to maintain sobriety and grow as a person, his sin of pride would have to be overcome. This happened through a profound Christian conversion. Then the man began to work on humility and found himself becoming a very humble person. However, the temptation of pride was still so much with him that he realized that he was beginning to develop pride in his humility! If he had let this happen, his would have been a restrictive Christian conversion, but, through daily prayer and surrender, he has avoided this temptation.

The research showed that the sin of pride is found in both male and female alcoholics. The responses of the women in the sampling suggest that the dynamics of conversion are similar in men and women. The women spoke of alcoholic pride in the same sense as the men.

The Case of Mr. Wright. Restrictive Christian conversion can be illustrated with the case of Mr. Wright, an active, late-middle-aged man who has been sober for over twenty years. His father died when Mr. Wright was seven years old. The family had no relationship to a church. The income was very low. Mr. Wright left home and wandered around the country as an adolescent. With a deprived background, this man, like the above alcoholic, was an ambition-ridden self. He was physically strong and had been a professional athlete. In the process of brilliant starts and sudden failures, Mr. Wright became an alcoholic. His wife was a Christian. He would have little to do with her religion. His hostility grew, until, as he says, he hated everybody. He came home drunk one night and struck his wife. This confronted him with the shock of reality and he began to cry in shame and sorrow. He said: " Lord, I want to be a Christian. If you will take the drink habit away from me, I will do anything you want." In that moment, Mr. Wright was converted. He has not had a drink since then, and that was over twenty years ago.

Mr. Wright became very successful in his business and extremely active in his religious life. His habitual and compulsive nature as an alcoholic can be seen in his life as a Christian. He takes *pride* in the fact that he refuses to make a business contract with anyone who deals in the sale of alcohol, and that he will not employ anyone who is a known drinker. He has little use for Alcoholics Anonymous, saying that only a Christian experience like his will solve the alcohol problem. He follows rigid religious rules for himself, which gives him a proud sense of superiority. He is presently as involved in his conversion experience as he was when it happened. He acts as if the twenty intervening years had not passed. His is a " static salvation " that is based on a perfectionistic, works-righteousness theology. He cannot relate to authoritative figures who would disagree with him.

In addition to being an ambition-ridden self, Mr. Wright is a " suspicious self," a system characterized by Wayne E. Oates as one who " does not feel as rejected as he feels deceived." [28] This man is the only person who became suspicious of the research procedure and refused to answer specific questions about his past. He is the kind of person who " sees himself as being totally right at all times, and seeks to determine the total course of life about him." [29] His suspicions do not come to the surface until he is pressed or confronted, so that in the usual routines of daily life, this man is happy and successful.

Characteristics of Restrictive Conversion. Salzman gives six characteristics that describe restrictive conversion. They are outlined as follows:

1. An exaggerated, irrational intensity of belief.
2. More concern with the form and doctrine than with the greater principle of belief.
3. Contempt and hatred toward former belief.
4. Intolerance toward all deviates, with the denouncing of previous friends and associates.
5. A crusading zeal and a need to involve others by seeking new converts.
6. Display of a need for martyrdom and self-punishment.[30]

These are not rigid rules of what one must be to be a restricted Christian convert. Most alcoholics who fall into this category probably, like Mr. Wright, are people who indicate low to moderate degrees of some of these characteristics. In many areas of life they may be very productive persons.

However, they portray, in a lesser way, the characteristics of the fanatical extremists who are also in this category. The fanatics are characterized by the " hellfire and damnation " preaching of ex-drunks who have learned to use religion compulsively as their escape, instead of alcohol. Eric Hoffer describes these " fiercest fanatics " as deprived, selfish people who have lost faith in themselves.

> They separate the excellent instrument of their selfishness from their ineffectual selves and attach it to the service of some holy cause. And though it be a faith of love and humility they adopt, they can be neither loving nor humble.[31]

Like psychosocial conversion, restrictive Christian conversion is an incomplete experience. The basis of human sin, pride, has not been converted. It has been redirected into a more socially acceptable and self-enhancing channel. This restricts the individual from grasping the full releasing grace of true Christianity. As Earl H. Furgeson has pointed out, it cannot be assumed that all conversions result in continuous growth and progress.[32] The restrictive elements of conversion can be recognized and dealt with for what they are.

III. LIMITED CHRISTIAN CONVERSION

The clinical research revealed a third category: *limited Christian conversion*. This category is similar to the restrictive conversion, but it is a separate and unique conversion pattern. There is a consciousness of sin, an expressed need for God's help, and a turning toward God. However, the individual's experience is one of intellectual belief and not personal commitment. He is an uncommitted person who believes in higher values but cannot give himself to these higher values. He either cannot or does not surrender himself totally to the new way of life he has affirmed intellectually. This may cause him to lead a double existence. On the one hand, he may attend church each Sunday and hold a position of responsibility in the church. On the other hand, his life during the week does not reflect religious principles. An alcoholic with a limited Christian conversion may drink during the week and stay sober on the weekends. He works hard at keeping up a good image.

Anton Boisen characterizes limited Christian conversion as *moderate religious concern*. Boisen describes the individual whose religious concern is moderate as one whose spiritual moods are transient and often inappropriate. He makes feeble attempts to act on the basis of religious teaching, such as attendance at church or certain private devotional rituals, but his " religion remains on the whole rather formal and superficial." [33] He is not a legalist with a proud display of spiritual arrogance, as is the restricted Christian convert. Rather, he is a guilt-ridden person who knows better but does not do better. He may revert to sentimental religious expression that is indicative of spiritual confusion rather than spiritual depth.

Self-systems in Limited Conversion. Two kinds of self-systems, as described by Oates, characterize the limited Christian convert. The first is " the dependent self," the person who is " persistently inadequate in all sorts of situations." [34] This person has not discovered his own selfhood. He lives on the goodness of others. He has trouble making decisions that vitally affect his own life. He procrastinates until someone makes the decision for him. Then he is likely to blame the other person for the consequences. Dependent persons are " often indecisive about 'what is right and wrong' and are equally indecisive about 'what they want to do with their lives,' 'what they believe about religion,' and the like." [35] The alcoholic who experiences a limited

Christian conversion may see himself as a " good person " who has had a " raw deal " in life.

The second self-system that applies to limited Christian conversion is " the despairing self," whose " personal resources for living have been depleted." [36] The person has had a meaningful religious experience, but he does not find resources in his religion to change his way of life from frustration to joy. Since he knows what is right but is unable to commit himself to it, his only alternative is despair. His religion is a burden rather than a release. He is confronted with spiritual realities he cannot attain. While the restricted Christian convert has an overabundance of self-love, the limited convert does not have enough. If the despair of the limited Christian convert goes unchecked, it may lead him into a form of mental illness. [37]

Anton Boisen maintains that when a person experiences a crisis in which he undergoes severe stress and inner conflict, he may become involved in one of two experiences that have similar dynamics. He may experience a religious conversion or he may regress into chronic mental illness. The difference between these two experiences is in the outcome.

> Where the outcome is destructive or inconclusive, we think of it as mental disorder. Where, on the other hand, it results in progressive unification and social adaptation we may think of it as religious experience. [38]

As Boisen has pointed out, a clear line of distinction cannot be drawn between these two experiences. The category of limited Christian conversion contains characteristics of both experiences. It is neither completely pathological nor completely healthy. It lies on the brink of both, where it may remain or go either way.

The Case of Mr. Cole. Limited Christian conversion is illustrated by the case of Mr. Cole, a lower-class, fifty-nine-year-old male. Mr. Cole's father was completely paralyzed by a stroke when Mr. Cole was four years old. The mother took over all the duties of running the household. As the thirteenth of fifteen children, Mr. Cole had little responsibility. He joined the church at the age of ten. He began automobile racing at the age of seventeen and became rather successful as a driver. However, at the age of twenty he began to drink, and, within a few years, lost his ability to race successfully. He and his wife opened their own business, but his alcoholism progressed. During this time he maintained a relationship with the church and even taught a Sunday school class. After World War II, Mr. Cole's alcoholism reached its worst stage. His wife separated from him for two years, during which time he remained isolated and drunk. He gave up all responsibility. One night he thought he was going to die. He asked God for help and verbally committed himself to God and sobriety. He lived through the night and experienced a Christian conversion through that crisis. Although he had been a church member for many years, this was Mr. Cole's first real conversion. It was the first time he had consciously turned to God for deliverance and made a commitment to him.

Mr. Cole remained sober for about five years. During this time he went back to his church and was reunited with his wife. However, he took a drink after work one day and came home drunk. Since that time his drinking has been periodic, as well as his relationship to the church. He did not keep his commitment to remain sober. Although he continues to drink and become intoxicated from time to time, Mr. Cole clings to his conversion experience as the turning point in his life. He talks of his religious experience with much sentimentality. Whenever he speaks of a tender subject he begins to cry. His emotional instability and immaturity indicate chronic brain damage, which, in itself, would limit his capacity for change. He is a very dependent person who lacks a concrete self-identity. His wife provides most of the income and is very domineering. In spite of his wife's aggressive dominance over him, Mr. Cole speaks of her with sentimental gratitude and affection, as though she could do no wrong. He lacks spiritual depth, but he tries to present a pious picture of himself.

In this case, it is quite possible that the individual changed as much as his capacity allowed. He is a weak person who has serious emotional handicaps. For him, a limited conversion was the best he could do. William James shows his sensitivity toward the individual and his acceptance of human experience by pointing out the validity of this kind of handicapped conversion. He says that the important thing is the meaning the conversion has for the individual, regardless of individual differences. James's sensitivity is seen in this statement:

> A small man's salvation will always be a great salvation and the greatest of all facts *for him*. . . . Who knows how much less ideal still the lives of these spiritual grubs and earthworms, these Crumps and Stigginses, might have been, if such poor grace as they have received had never touched them at all? [39]

Walter Houston Clark correctly points out that James, through his careful study of human nature and experience, saw the fruits of religious experience as good.[40] Therefore, the person whose capacity for change does not extend beyond a limited Christian conversion is not beyond " a great salvation." He is handicapped, but not rejected. A limited conversion may be valid for the person who has it.

The Case of Mr. Kemp. Another case illustrates, however, the fact that for some individuals a limited conversion is incomplete. It does not reach the limits of their capacity for change. This can be seen in the case of Mr. Kemp, aged thirty-nine. Mr. Kemp began to drink at the age of sixteen, had become a heavy drinker at the age of twenty-five, and was an alcoholic within two or three years. At the age of thirty, Mr. Kemp attended a Billy Graham rally with his wife, who was a Presbyterian. He had been a Roman Catholic. Both of them felt a deep spiritual impact at the meeting.

When the invitation was given, they "went forward." Mr. Kemp accepted Jesus Christ as his Savior and experienced a Christian conversion. He was enthusiastic about the experience and went back the next day for counseling. He was encouraged by Graham to join a church. The next Sunday he and his wife joined the local Presbyterian church. Mr. Kemp affirms the presence of the Holy Spirit in this experience and reports that he felt very deeply about what he was doing.

After his conversion, Mr. Kemp became active in his church. He taught a Sunday school class. However, his drinking did not stop. It became worse. He was drunk five nights out of the week. He says, " I loved alcohol more than I loved the Lord." He led a double life — drunk during the week and sober on the weekend. He forced himself to stay sober on the weekend so that he could teach his Sunday school class and keep up his respectable image. He thought no one knew of his excessive drinking. His conversion was a limited Christian conversion. He had acknowledged principles of belief, but he had not surrendered to these principles, assimilated them into his life, and put them into the practice of living. There was no personal commitment. There was only intellectual affirmation. As another alcoholic said, he had " believed but not *accepted* what he believed." Acceptance was seen by this alcoholic as applying belief to daily acts. There was little or no application of Christian truth to Mr. Kemp's life. He had a superficial faith with moderate religious concern.

Following an automobile accident in which, while drunk, he narrowly escaped serious injury or death, Mr. Kemp began to wonder what purpose God had for his life. He saw his escape as a " miracle " in which God had spared him. However, his alcoholic drinking continued. He was threatened with divorce by his wife. He finally went to a psychiatrist, but he lied to the doctor. Suddenly one morning, after being drunk the night before, Mr. Kemp got up and told his wife he had taken his last drink. He confessed his powerlessness over alcohol and said he would never take a drink again. This act of surrender took place spontaneously and almost unconsciously. Mr. Kemp says he was not sure what made him say it, but he knew he meant it. He says that it was not himself speaking at all, but God speaking through him. Alone, he would not have been able to surrender and really mean it. That was in 1962, and Mr. Kemp has lived a sober, happy, and productive life since then.

Mr. Kemp moved from a limited Christian conversion to a comprehensive Christian conversion. He had continued to be a despairing self through his six years of drinking after his conversion. It was not until he had fulfilled his capacity for change that he became a complete self under God which was "unified and consciously right, superior, and happy, in consequence of its firmer hold upon religious realities." [41] His giving up alcohol, an alcoholic's most precious possession, was the sign of total surrender to the will of God.

IV. COMPREHENSIVE CHRISTIAN CONVERSION

In each of the preceding categories of conversion, there are aspects that indicate the incompleteness of the conversion. There is something present in each experience that hinders a total, all-inclusive change in the individual. The full fruits of conversion are not allowed to develop. The growth process is blocked, either temporarily or permanently. Therefore, there is a fourth category of conversion that is not hindered by "the damming up of the way to a life of free and self-giving love." [42] This is *comprehensive Christian conversion*. The term "comprehensive" is used to convey the sense of being deeply felt, total, transforming, releasing, and transcendent. Comprehensive conversion is genuine conversion. It emphasizes the central focus of life around the revelation of God in Jesus Christ. It involves a total response of faith and not a partial response of either religious hyperactivity or spiritual inertia. As an experience with holistic dimensions, it breaks the power of compulsion, both to alcohol and the legalism of proud religiosity.

Comprehensive Christian conversion is similar to what Henry Nelson Wieman and Regina Westcott-Wieman call " supreme conversion," characterized as

> that reorganization of the personality which enables one to live for those unexplored possibilities which transcend all time but are nevertheless possibilities of existence because they can be approximated to an indefinite degree by reason of the indeterminate nature of existence, and through the growth of meaning.[43]

What the Wiemans leave out and what is included here is the need for a " cornerstone " upon which God builds and around which a man can mobilize his personal strengths for purposeful living.

Dynamic Salvation. David E. Roberts refers to this category of conversion in his discussion of " a dynamic view of salvation." [44] He says that " salvation should be thought of primarily in terms of a dynamic transformation that removes man-made evils at the source by changing the man." [45] Here is the holistic approach to salvation. It is an experience that involves the whole man, not some of his parts. Comprehensive and genuine conversion is a dynamic process. It involves rebirth and growth. The person feels both freedom and commitment, the power of personal action, and the presence of God in the fellowship of the Holy Spirit.

Since this is the category of Christian conversion toward which all men should strive, it is essential to adopt characteristics of this comprehensive experience that may serve as criteria of validity. Herbert A. Tyson suggests a simple formula of three characteristics of valid religious experience:

1. The self experienced as shared: openness and identity.
2. The self experienced as honest: " truth-telling " and " leveling."
3. The self experienced as worth while: equality and belonging.[46]

Self-consistency. Implicit in Tyson's formula is Prescott Lecky's theory of self-consistency. Lecky proposes to " apprehend all psychological phenomena as illustrations of the single principle of unity or self-consistency." [47] The personality is seen as an organization of values that are consistent with one another, but that revolve around two sets of problems:

> one the problem of maintaining inner harmony within himself, and the other the problem of maintaining harmony with the environment, especially the social environment, in the midst of which he lives.[48]

Self-consistency is subjective rather than objective. " It is the organization of experience into an integrated whole." [49] The individual with a comprehensive Christian conversion maintains harmony within himself through honesty and a sense of worth. He maintains harmony with his environment through sharing himself, with his own identity, in an open relationship with others. His self-consistency is maintained through his personal faith in God and his fellowship with those who share his faith. Anton Boisen states that

> consistency in the sense of increasing harmony in the internal organization, together with increasing adjustment to the external world, is an important criterion in the validation of any belief or system of belief.[50]

András Angyal speaks of this in terms of the " trend toward autonomy " and the " trend toward homonomy." [51]

Characteristics of Comprehensive Conversion. Drawing from Gordon W. Allport's discussion of the mature religious sentiment,[52] Samuel Southard has listed six characteristics of a " fruitful conversion ":

1. *A Christ-like conversion experience is well defined.*
2. *A maturing conversion is full of life.*
3. *A fruitful conversion produces a consistent morality.*

4. *The mature conversion is comprehensive.*
5. *Each part of a man's religious experience is closely connected to every other part.*
6. *The mature convert is a humble learner.*[53]

Southard says that the mature conversions are "the source of the theological and psychological characteristics of a shift in loyalty toward Jesus Christ." [54] Comprehensive Christian conversion reveals itself by its fruits.

The Principle of Linkage. The interrelatedness of these characteristics is underscored by Daniel Day Williams with his "principle of 'linkage' in human existence." [55] Man is a whole being, but he is also made up of parts. As a creature of God, man "is the being who finds every part of his experience linked with every other part." [56] This principle points out the significance that giving up alcohol has for the alcoholic. This act is linked with every other act he performs. It is the giving up of a part of his life, alcohol, that affects every other part. To maintain his drinking, to any extent, would produce a weak link in the chain of his experience. It also points out the spiritual significance of the struggle with alcohol. Such a struggle "may become the focal point of the wrestle of the soul with God." [57] The mere act of trying to gain sobriety may lead an alcoholic to a genuine Christian conversion.

The Case of Mrs. Simmons. The case of Mrs. Simmons illustrates comprehensive Christian conversion. This middle-aged mother of three children is divorced and works as a secretary. Her father deserted the family when she was eight. She attended the Baptist church with her mother. Mrs. Simmons' drinking began when she was nineteen. Drinking reduced her inferiority feelings and social inadequacy. She had become an alcoholic by the age of thirty-nine, after her divorce. Before the divorce, she, her husband, and the children joined the Episcopal church. In her last five years of drinking, life became much worse. A neighbor described her as withdrawn and unfriendly. She continued

to attend church when she was sober, but it had little meaning for her. Knowing she needed help, she contacted Alcoholics Anonymous and began to attend meetings. After
five months she was still drinking and felt hopeless. A sense
of sin drove her to despair. In desperation, she called an
older man in Alcoholics Anonymous and asked him what she
should do. He advised her to pray openly to God for help.
She prayed for two days. As long as she prayed, she could resist the compulsion to drink, but the desire was very strong.
The next morning she drove to work, not knowing whether
her job was there or not. As she was driving she continued
to pray for God's help. Suddenly she was filled with a sense
of assurance. She felt the impact of God's presence. For the
first time she was filled with an inner sense of confidence.
She surrendered herself to God and opened herself to his
help. New hope flooded her life. She became a different person and has not had a drink in four years. Mrs. Simmons is
able to say explicitly how her life has changed since her
conversion. She finds a new depth of meaning in church,
prayer, and devotion. Her spiritual life grows daily. She relates happily and meaningfully to others. She demonstrates
a deeply affectionate relationship to her children. When her
name is mentioned in a group of her acquaintances, a common response is, " Isn't she a wonderful person? " Relatively
few people know that she is an alcoholic, even though she is
very active in Alcoholics Anonymous. She lives a full life,
practicing what she calls " creative sobriety." By this she
means not making sobriety one's life goal, but realizing that
one's goals will not be attained without it. She expresses
deep gratitude to God for her deliverance from alcohol. This
is reflected in her genuine humility.

The Case of Mrs. Dunn. Another such quiet, but sudden,
experience occurred in the life of Mrs. Dunn. This late-
middle-aged businesswoman had grown up in a home with
rigid religious concepts. This was especially true of the
mother, who was very judgmental and critical of others.
The father was more open. The family belonged to the

Christian church. Mrs. Dunn began to drink at the age of thirty-three. She became an alcoholic within a year, becoming addicted very quickly. She was an ambitious person who had high goals for herself. After a divorce, she began to go to night school while working each day. It was during this time that she became an alcoholic. She continued to go to church to try to project a good image. She remarried, and her second husband was a problem drinker himself. However, when he saw what alcohol was doing to her, he stopped drinking, hoping she would stop too.

Finally, Mrs. Dunn hit bottom. She lost all self-respect. One morning she was home, alone, drinking. She felt miserable and hopeless. Her hair was untidy and she had on an old dirty robe. Her face was swollen and her eyes bloodshot. She went into the bathroom and looked in the mirror. Suddenly, she saw herself and realized what she had become. She felt numb. She fell to her knees in an act of surrender and prayed, " Here I am, Lord, do with me what you will." Immediately after that she began to feel better. She felt that real hope had come into her life. The room seemed filled with the Holy Spirit. She quietly went to her bedroom and got dressed. Then she called the Alcoholics Anonymous office and found where a meeting would be held that night. From that time on, Mrs. Dunn has been a new person. She is active in Alcoholics Anonymous. She holds a position of responsibility in her local church and in the state convention. Her relationship with God has grown deeper in the years since her conversion. She is an open person who seeks to learn more about herself. She is a competent person who has gained the respect of others. Her comprehensive conversion has led her into a full life.

Charles Stinnette calls such an experience " the shock of recognition." [58] Reality came to Mrs. Dunn in the shock of recognition. She looked in the mirror and saw herself as she really was — estranged from self and God. She saw deeper than her disheveled appearance. She saw the emptiness of her soul. " The shock of recognition fulfills its proper function when in recalling us to ourselves it prepares us for . . . openness to change." [59] Mrs. Dunn expressed her openness through surrender. Stinnette names *contrition* as the religious attitude that conveys this openness to change. " The work of grace in searching our heart is directed toward the transformation of a broken spirit into a contrite heart." [60]

The Case of Mr. Grant. The comprehensive conversion may be either sudden or gradual. A gradual experience was reported by Mr. Grant, a middle-class Methodist. This man had become addicted to alcohol by the age of fifty. When he tried to stop drinking, he could not. He became frightened. He thought he was a hopeless alcoholic and wanted to die. He tried to get his wife to divorce him, but she refused to leave. She told him she was praying for him. He had attended church occasionally, but in his worst years of drinking he withdrew completely.

Finally, in desperation, he went to Alcoholics Anonymous. He attended his first meeting drunk. After that he went faithfully for a year. In this experience he became aware of his deep spiritual needs. He began to read meditation books. Prayer became a part of his daily life. He found new meaning in his church. God became a reality to him. On one occasion he read Eph. 2:1-8 and was struck by the words, " For by grace you have been saved through faith; and this is not your own doing, it is the gift of God." In the light of this verse he understood his own experience. God, through his grace, had saved him from destruction by alcohol. Mr. Grant says that the realization of this fact was his most meaningful spiritual experience. He is now active in his church and in Alcoholics Anonymous. He holds a position of responsibility in his church. He is a quiet person who relates warmly to others. His Christian conversion has been a gradual process rather than a sudden experience.

The clinical data reveal that William James was correct in defining conversion as either gradual or sudden and related to the process of growth. Growth may take place in the sudden burst of emotional upheaval, or in the unfolding awareness of one's deepest needs. Furgeson's concept that conversion has no relationship to the natural processses of growth ignores human experience.[61] It assumes that religious conversion is something that is added on to human nature rather than being intrinsic to it. Through comprehensive Christian conversion the way is open for unrestricted personal and spiritual growth.

CHAPTER III

Dynamics of Christian Experience in Alcoholism

THE CONVERSION of the alcoholic is a directional shift or change of nature in the individual's life. When this experience is examined microscopically, it becomes apparent that just as an atom is composed of many molecules, conversion is composed of many facets. These motivating and energizing facets are called the dynamics of Christian experience. This chapter delineates and examines some of these dynamics in alcoholism.

I. THE VARIETY OF CONVERSION EXPERIENCES

Even within the four categories of conversion, there are varieties of experiences. Individual differences condition religious experience. Edgar Y. Mullins recognized this by writing that

> there are many varieties in the experience of those who find Christ. The point of emphasis varies with the individual. With some, love seems to be the dominating motive. With others, it is obedience, with others, hope; and in some cases merely the desire to do right is the chief motive.[1]

Samuel Southard notes that age, personality, and theological teaching are among the factors that condition religious experience.[2] A child who has been nurtured in the church may find his religious experience to be a normal part of his development. Whether it has or does not have significant meaning for the child, it is not likely to be a highly emotional experience. An exception to this, however, would be in those groups where ecstatic emotion *must* accompany religious conversion. An adult, on the other hand, experiences disruption of set patterns and ideas that may cause him to erupt in an upsurge of emotion. Persons with a more suggestible personality will tend to be conditioned by the external circumstances of their conversion. Theological teaching sets expectations for conversion patterns. An individual's experience is conditioned by how he thinks that experience should be expressed.

The clinical material revealed the varieties of Christian conversion in alcoholism. Eleven individuals of the research sampling indicated sudden experiences. Nine indicated gradual conversions. A sudden conversion does not necessarily mean a highly emotional experience. It means that the individual can refer to a specific moment and point out how his life was changed in that moment. The emotional tone of the moment may have been either quiet or violent. For example, one woman, in desperation, prayed one night that God would deliver her from alcohol. In her prayer she opened herself to God. As a result, she felt a peace she had never known before. She relaxed, knowing there was hope. It was a quiet, but sudden experience. Another alcoholic came home drunk and hit his wife. In the suddenness of his shame and guilt, he asked God to help him. His experience was accompanied with an outbreak of crying and uncontrolled emotion.

The gradual experiences were processes of searching for help from God. No outbreaks of emotion were involved. For example, one man, highly educated, found sobriety through Alcoholics Anonymous. Within a few weeks after he entered that fellowship, he felt a deep need for a Christian conversion. He began to try to assimilate into his life the beliefs that he had previously intellectually affirmed. He read the Bible and prayed daily. He listened carefully in church. He tried to deal with others in the spirit of love. In the process he found his spiritual needs being met. His Christian experience became deeply meaningful and his life peaceful and happy.

The balance, in the sampling, of sudden and gradual conversions confirms the widely held theory that both types are valid conversion experiences. " The main point," says Mullins, " is that individuals differ in the accent of experience. Human nature has a great range of emotion and a great range of need." [3] This range is indicated in the twenty cases in this study. Writing in 1920, James B. Pratt said that conversion may be expressed in different ways,

> but the . . . only essential part of it is just this new birth by which a man ceases to be a mere psychological thing or a divided self and becomes a unified being with a definite direction under the guidance of a group of consistent and harmonious purposes or ideals. [4]

In Christian conversion, one essential must be made explicit. That is, a growing faith in the revelation of God in Jesus Christ.

II. Pride and Humility

The discussion of restrictive Christian conversion, in Chapter II, indicated the problem of pride in the experience of alcoholism. The clinical evidence supports Niebuhr's concept that pride is the basis of human sin. [5] It also indicates that it is only when the alcoholic can generate genuine humility that he becomes a sober and free person. Genuine humility is a mark of comprehensive Christian conversion.

The alcoholic is like the neurotic, described by Karen Horney as lacking what he needs most — self-confidence and self-respect. [6] He is filled with feelings of inferiority and social inadequacy. These feelings may go back to childhood and the drinking may be an attempt to relieve them. Because of the pain of low self-esteem, the alcoholic erects an almost impenetrable defense — neurotic pride. " Neurotic pride . . . rests on the attributes which a person arrogates to himself in his imagination, on all those belonging to his particular idealized image." [7]

The pride of the alcoholic is bound up in unsubstantiated attributes that reflect glorification of himself. His egocentricity has been lifted to the " dignity of a life philosophy." [8] His pride is a false pride with which he deceives only himself. Denial of reality becomes an unconscious way of life. Whenever his false pride is threatened, the alcoholic finds a way to save face. Many who are church members continue to go to church to " keep up appearances." They will usually arrive at church late and leave early so that they can be seen at a distance, but not up close. Thus, the alcoholic builds up an elaborate " system of avoidances," an unconscious process to protect himself from those situations where he may be exposed.[9] Reinhold Niebuhr echoes this concept when he says, " It would not be inaccurate to define the first purpose of intoxication as the sinful ego-assertion which is rooted in anxiety and unduly compensates for the sense of inferiority and insecurity. . . ." [10]

Horney points out that pride and self-hate belong inseparably together. She refers to the factors involved in this one process as " the pride system." This system is derived from a dissociation of the actual self from the ideal self. The alcoholic hates himself as he actually is. This hate is so painful that he does not even allow himself to think about it. He refuses to look at his actual self and, instead, sees himself as he would like to be — his ideal self. However, his attempts to be what he is not end in failure, and alcohol is his only escape. The *actual self* becomes the victim of the *ideal self*. No matter which way the alcoholic turns, he cannot avoid pain. Pain demands relief, and alcohol is always available. The only hope for him is the emergence of the real self to do battle and overcome the ideal self. The alcoholic's real self begins to emerge when his false pride shows signs of weakening and alcohol is causing him more anguish than relief. It is a life-and-death struggle, but the pride system must be shattered if the real self, with its freedom of decision and assumption of responsibility, comes into being.[11]

The pride of the alcoholic must be replaced with genuine humility. As mentioned earlier, this is not an easy task, and it requires a comprehensive conversion. Erich Fromm, discussing the Roman Catholic Church, points out the pitfalls encountered when narcissism is involved. He says that

> while the omniscience and omnipotence of God should have led to man's humility, often the individual identified himself with God and thus developed an extraordinary degree of narcissism in this process of identification.[12]

This identification marks the superiority of the ideal self and prohibits the attitude of humility. Genuine humility is characterized by gratitude toward God, recognition of one's limitations (such as powerlessness over alcohol), openness and sensitivity toward others, and dedication to being oneself.

III. The Meaning of Surrender

A common experience shared by the alcoholics in the sampling was the experience of surrender. It was through surrender that they found sobriety. The surrender phenomenon is essential to the experience of total conversion. It, like conversion, may be a gradual or a sudden surrender. To use Horney's terms, it is the event or process in which the proud *ideal self* is shattered and the *real self* emerges into a dominant position in the personality. It is the turning from self-destruction to self-realization.

The Necessity of Surrender. Harry M. Tiebout strongly

emphasizes the necessity of surrender as a prerequisite to conversion. A converted alcoholic, he says,

> after trying to manage his own case to his own near ruination, . . . gave up the bottle and surrendered to the need for help, after which he entered a new state of mind which has enabled him to remain sober.[18]

Defiant individuality and grandiosity block surrender. These must be overcome. Surrender is defined as

> a moment when the unconscious forces of defiance and grandiosity actually cease to function effectively. When that happens the individual is wide open to reality; he can listen and learn without conflict and fighting back.[14]

This spiritual event is demonstrated vividly in the case of Mr. Wright, described in Chapter II, whose defiance and grandiosity were shattered when he, who had been a professional athlete, had degenerated to the point of hitting a woman. This shattering made surrender possible. However, grandiosity was later associated with his conversion experience and genuine humility remained absent. His ideal physical self was converted to an ideal spiritual self. Alcoholic pride was changed to spiritual pride. Mr. Wright experienced an *act* of surrender, but he did not follow through with what Tiebout calls a *state* of surrender. The state of surrender is the persisting capacity to accept reality without obligation or fatalism. It combines courage with humility.

The case of Mrs. Mills demonstrates the state of surrender. This middle-aged woman is in her third marriage to the third alcoholic. She has been an alcoholic for over ten years. She has been hospitalized for alcoholism at a state mental hospital and for cirrhosis of the liver in a general hospital. After four years in Alcoholics Anonymous she was still drinking. In her last hospitalization, she began to recognize her spiritual needs. In a gradual process she surrendered herself to God. For the first time she gained a personal faith. Her state of surrender can be seen in a recent experience.

When she lost her second husband by suicide, Mrs. Mills completely broke down and stayed drunk for weeks, to escape the grief and frustration. Just a few weeks before the research interview, Mrs. Mills's present husband attempted suicide. This was very upsetting to her, and she was tempted to drink. However, she tried to pray instead of drinking. She prayed for God's help and assurance. Her dependence upon God enabled her to move through this experience without turning to alcohol. She faced reality with new courage and strength. She followed her *act* of surrender with a *state* of surrender. Tiebout combines both into a single phenomenon that he calls the " surrender reaction."

Tiebout points out that for some

> there seems to occur a phenomenon which might be called " selective surrender." After the effects of the initial surrender experience have worn away, the individual reverts to being much the same person he was before, except that he does not drink and so has no battle on that line.[15]

This is characteristic of the restrictive Christian conversion. " Selective surrender " was seen in the case of Mr. Wright, who remains compulsive and habitual in his dependence upon the rituals of the religious life.

Surrender and Submission. There is an important distinction between surrender and submission. Tiebout indicates that submission is a conscious, superficial yielding in which tension continues. To refer again to Angyal's term, submission may be thought of as a " part-process " that disrupts the total functioning of the person.[16] It is partial rather than total. Submission is a halfhearted, tension-producing expression that denies the need for a totally functioning personality. Surrender, on the other hand, is wholehearted, unconscious, and provides release from tension.

The case of Mr. Kemp, referred to in Chapter II, illustrates the difference between submission and surrender. In his initial conversion experience, Mr. Kemp submitted to Billy Graham's persuasive invitation, but he continued to drink and feel unhappy and sad. It was not until he surrendered six years later that he became sober and experienced peace and joy. The late András Angyal said:

> Submission and surrender both refer to a state of non-assertion of individuality, of losing oneself in something else, but the difference is momentous. One submits to the alien and becomes diminished through submission; one surrenders one's isolation to enter into a larger unit and enlarges one's life.[17]

Submission is characteristic of limited Christian conversion. Surrender is characteristic of comprehensive Christian conversion.

The Paradox of Surrender. The " surrender reaction " is paradoxical in nature. Alcoholism is a battle that can be won only by giving up. It has to be more than a compromising self-negotiation. Unconditional surrender in the face of the reality of defeat will, alone, bring victory. Martin D. Kissen says that surrender involves the recognition of powerlessness over alcohol.

> This, of course, implies rather paradoxically that the only way to defeat the consequences of alcoholism is to surrender to the fact that he cannot ingest any alcohol.[18]

Edgar Y. Mullins put it in theological language by saying that when a person surrenders to Jesus Christ, his natural potential is released and

> he is put in the way of complete self-realization by faith in Christ. This is what Jesus means by the saying: " He that findeth his life shall lose it; and he that loseth his life for my sake shall find it." [19]

The alcoholic must surrender more than alcohol. Alcohol must be a part of his surrender, but his surrender will not be effective unless it is a total response of *himself*.

IV. The Sense of Shame and Sin

Although Tiebout speaks at length about the "surrender reaction" of the alcoholic when he faces reality and accepts it, he does not explore the deeper emotional state that preconditions surrender. Eight cases in the research sampling indicated that a primary feeling before their surrender was the sense of *shame*. Shame confronted the alcoholics with reality and shattered their ideal self. It made them see themselves as they really were. Their self-image was unaligned with their behavior. This split revealed their lack of identity, real or pseudo. Unable to mobilize any defense against utter shame, the alcoholic had no real alternative except surrender.

Russell L. Dicks noted that the alcoholic comes equipped with a sense of shame. "The alcoholic has low self-esteem, loss of a sense of personhood, loss of a sense of dignity." [20] Feeling threatened and defensive, the individual retreats into the hard shell of alcoholism. He cannot think much of others when he thinks so little of himself. His suspicious attitude toward others reflects his own basic mistrust in himself. Shame and trust are poles apart.

Abraham H. Maslow, professor of psychology at Brandeis University, states that those who do not live up to their potential and who betray themselves "perceive in a deep way that they have done wrong to themselves and despise themselves for it." [21] Out of this experience will come either neurosis or growth and renewal of courage and self-respect. To despise oneself is to possess a deep, shattering sense of shame for oneself. One alcoholic demonstrated this reaction by trying to get his wife to divorce him because he was "no good."

A psychological understanding of shame has been enhanced by Helen Merrell Lynd. Much of what she says about the characteristics of shame applies to the conversion of an alcoholic. Lynd says:

> Being taken unpleasantly by surprise, the impossibility of ordered behavior, the sudden sense of exposure, of being unable to deal with what is happening, characterize shame. It is as if a self of which we were not aware makes us unable to grasp the situation and to control what we do.[22]

This sudden exposure is seen in the case of Mr. Goode, which was reported in Chapter II as a psychosocial conversion. He had seen himself as a decent, respectable person. In his experience of shame he saw himself being crude and disrespectful to a young woman. The suddenness of his exposure brought him to a spontaneous surrender. Since shame is a personal event involving the whole person, the only way it can be transcended is by the surrender of the whole person.

Lynd emphasizes the suddenness of shame, but the clinical research revealed shame as a process as well as an event. For example, one lady, Mrs. Ross, reported that her most profound feeling was her *shame* of being an alcoholic. She said, " I'd rather have been a leper than an alcoholic." As a defense against a growing sense of shame, Mrs. Ross constructed a " tremendous ego." Her case illustrates that self-contempt and pride may be two aspects of the same personality manifestation. Both are involved in the alcoholic's experience. The false pride of an ideal self kept her from admitting her alcoholism. Since Mrs. Ross was a " respectable " upper-middle-class person, no one mentioned to her the possibility of alcoholism, not even her psychiatrist. There was no sudden exposure, but an infiltration of shame. She became a very sad person. She could not accept her actual self; she could not trust her ideal self; and she could not identify her real self. Her abiding sense of shame preconditioned her surrender and subsequent Christian conversion and sobriety.

A Polish psychiatrist, Kazimierz Dabrowski, discusses the social aspects of shame. He sees shame as " the primary expression of sensitiveness to the judgment of the external world." [23] It expresses disharmony of internal and external moral values. Mrs. Ross's social class was probably a strong factor in her experience. John Dollard indicates that the upper-middle class has a neutral attitude toward drinking. However, its proximity to the lower-middle class, which has a strong taboo on drinking, makes recognition of alcoholism a very anxiety-producing experience.[24] Thus, Mrs. Ross's sense of shame would be increased by her social environment.

The religiously oriented person may interpret his sense of shame as an awareness of sin. Eight persons in the sampling listed *sin* as one of their primary feelings before their conversion. Seven of these had received some form of early religious training. This indicates that their perception of themselves tended to fall into religious categories. Therefore, shame would overlap into one's concept of sin.

Mullins viewed sin in its vertical and horizontal dimensions. He saw it basically as man's breach of a covenant relationship with God. This rupture also involves man's relationship with his fellowman. Sin is idolatry, falsehood, injustice, insincerity, and guile. Fundamentally, sin is characterized by " the bent of our nature " rather than " our separate acts." [25]

A broader view of sin is given by Marc Oraison. Drawing from Paul's discussion of sin in Rom., chs. 7 and 8, Oraison outlines the Christian psychology of sin. " First of all, we are aware of sin only because the Law has made it known to us." [26] This is the vertical dimension of sin. It is man's recognition of his responsibility for higher values. It involves man's covenant relationship with God. " Second, we must note the interior division, which is both universal and dramatic, introduced by this awareness." [27] This involves man's inner conflict, the inability to make satisfying decisions and to see them through. It is spiritual anarchy within the self. Thirdly, " sin corresponds to an existential situation that is both social and personal: the division between the dynamism of love and adherence to illusions of false values." [28] The man who experiences social conflict also experiences inner conflict. This view of sin indicates its similarity to shame. Both involve conflict with higher values, with interpersonal relationships, and within the self.

Guilt is also involved in the feelings of the alcoholic. He may feel guilty for many things. However, guilt incorporates much less of the total sense of exposure and emptiness that characterizes shame and sin. Therefore, the alcoholic's experience of surrender and conversion is best understood in the comprehensive, dynamic terms of shame and sin. These feelings serve to shatter the alcoholic's illusions about himself and leave him open to conversion.

V. The Role of Confession and Forgiveness

The sense of shame and sin leads to conversion through the act of confession. Seward Hiltner has noted that most Protestant churches have tended " to deal with confession and assurance of forgiveness on a more occasional and informal basis." [29] Protestants, while assuring men of forgiveness, have all but ignored confession. Confession is another experience shared by each of the alcoholics in the sampling. Prominent in their experience following their confession and subsequent conversion was the sense of forgiveness. Both confession and forgiveness had divine and human implications. Each confession was made in the presence of both God and a company of persons. In ten cases, a private confession to God preceded a public confession. In the remaining ten cases, no real distinction could be made between the confession before God and the confession before men. However, in the latter cases, there was a consciousness of the presence of God as well as the presence of man.

Alcoholics Anonymous recognizes the value of open confession and encourages its members to confess on two main points. The first confession should be that of powerlessness over alcohol. However, for this to be effective, it must be followed by a deeper confession of the nature of their wrongdoing. This amounts to an open, honest, confession of sin. It must be made before God, self, and at least one other person if it is to effect a change in one's life and allow him to experience forgiveness.[30]

In only one case did the alcoholic make an open, public confession before a church congregation. This occurred in the experience of Mr. Roberts, a Negro Methodist. Even during his alcoholism, Mr. Roberts continued his relationship with his church. He was discouraged and dissatisfied with life. He says that when he was twenty, he felt God calling him to preach. He had tried to ignore and deny this feeling for seventeen years. His interpretation of his alcoholism is that it was an escape from God's call. His life was filled with despair and hopelessness. When he hit bottom, he decided that his only hope was to face squarely the call of God. He had reached the point of surrender. One Sunday night, Mr. Roberts stood behind the pulpit and faced the entire congregation. He confessed how he had attempted to avoid God's call and had turned to alcohol as a means of escape. He became very emotional and was able to say only a few sentences, but he "walked out of that church a free man." Mr. Roberts experienced divine and human forgiveness through his open confession.

Max Thurian underscores such experiences by saying that

> open-heartedness towards one another among the members of one and the same Church is one of the most important factors making for the realization in existence of the essential unity of the community.[31]

It is significant that Mr. Roberts had been a member of this church for almost twenty years. He was well known there and had a durable relationship with the people. He demonstrates that "openness between individuals can be made real in the sharing in common of the spiritual wealth of all, as well as the sharing of the difficulties encountered and the victories won." [32] Thurian, a Catholic priest who views confession sacramentally, sees this as "not confession properly so-called, but a simple exchange which saves the individual from becoming unhealthily wrapped up in the cult of his own personality." [33] The alcoholic does form a private "cult." Confession before a community delivers him from bondage to this "cult" and gives him freedom in forgiveness.

Another alcoholic found human forgiveness in a series of experiences, climaxed by a profound realization of divine forgiveness. Mr. Dixon, a middle-aged salesman, was in Alcoholics Anonymous for ten years before he became sober. The only "higher power" he knew during these years was the group itself. Through the kindness of recovered alcoholics, he began to trust a Power outside the group. His religious consciousness began to grow and he developed a genuine faith in God. Nevertheless, his sense of forgiveness remained on the human level. He did not feel God's forgiveness. In his spiritual growth he became sober. One drunken act of which he was particularly ashamed was his borrowing his father's car, selling it, and using the money for a "bender," a long drinking spree. This had hurt his father very deeply, but he had not reprimanded his adult son. After Mr. Dixon became sober, he and his father, a devout Catholic, developed a meaningful relationship, but he continued to feel guilty about the car incident although he had confessed his guilt.

At the time of his father's death, Mr. Dixon had been sober for a year and a half. Because he had been such a disappointment to his father for so many years, he expected to receive nothing from his father's estate. He knew no forgiveness that could go that far. However, he was overwhelmed when he heard the attorney read the will and repeat the deceased father's words, " If I have a car at the time of my death, I want it to go to my son, John." Mr. Dixon says that at that moment he understood the forgiveness of God. It must be unlimited. Since that time he has felt a closeness with God that has been deeply meaningful to him. He has been sober for over two years.

VI. The Loss and Recovery of Hope

Fifteen out of the twenty alcoholics in the sampling reported a definite feeling of utter hopelessness before their conversion. Seventeen reported either a recovered or a renewed sense of hope after their conversion. This is strong evidence that loss and recovery of hope is one of the most significant single dynamics in the conversion of an alcoholic.

Paul Pruyser states that hope is such a dynamic quality that it should be thought of, semantically, in the active connotation of " hoping " rather than the philosophical abstraction of " hope." He sees hoping as " an urge toward deliverance." [34] It is that human quality which, when activated, moves toward conversion and toward freedom.

The role of the hoping process in the alcoholic's experience is illuminated by Gabriel Marcel. Marcel maintains that true hope is not possible until one is faced with hopelessness.

> The truth is that there can strictly be no hope except when the temptation to despair exists. Hope is the act by which this temptation is actively or victoriously overcome.[35]

Hope is so real to the alcoholic because he is a prisoner of hopelessness. Alcoholism is a vicious cycle from which there seems to be no escape. It is existential imprisonment. Hope, if present at all, may be very dim. However,

> the soul always turns towards a light which it does not perceive, a light yet to be born, in the hope of being

> delivered from its present darkness, the darkness of waiting, a darkness which cannot be prolonged without dragging it in some way towards an organic dissolution.[36]

This quotation characterizes the progression of alcoholism from mental anguish to organic deterioration.

Absolute hope, says Marcel, springs only from encounter with that which is Absolute.

> It appears as a response of the creature to the infinite Being to whom it is conscious of owing everything that it has and upon whom it cannot impose any condition whatsoever without scandal.[37]

The case of Mr. Dixon illustrates this point. Ten years of active relationship with Alcoholics Anonymous did not deliver him from alcoholism until he found hope in a personal God and divine forgiveness. This same experience was evident in eight of the cases studied.

The essentiality of hope is supported by Erik Erikson, who sees it as " both the earliest and the most indispensable virtue inherent in the state of being alive." [38] He says that " if life is to be sustained hope must remain, even where confidence is wounded, trust impaired." [39] The individual who loses hope regresses into a kind of lifeless state. Life loses all meaning and purpose. Two cases studied indicated the planning of suicide when all hope was lost.

Erikson sees the origin of hope as relying on " trustworthy maternal persons," who affectionately meet the infant's basic needs. He seems to underestimate the paternal role in the infant's experience. Translated into the adult experience, both the maternal and paternal aspects of the formation of hope may be realized in dependency upon God as the source of hope. The individual, through prayer, is able to transcend his hopeless state and gain hope from outside of his own dark environment. The " religious sentiment induces adults to restore their hopefulness in periodic petitionary prayer, assuming a measure of child-likeness toward unseen, omnipotent powers." [40]

Emil Brunner begins his discussion of a theology of hope by comparing hope with the necessity for oxygen.

> Take oxygen away and death occurs through suffoca-
> tion, take hope away and humanity is constricted
> through lack of breath; despair supervenes, spelling
> the paralysis of intellectual and spiritual powers by a
> feeling of the senselessness and purposelessness of
> existence.[41]

Just as oxygen is essential to life, so is hope. The cases studied in this research validate Brunner's statement. Hope proved to be vital not only in the recovery from alcoholism, but also in the emergence of a new personality, a personality that found its freedom in healthy dependence upon a hope-giving God.

VII. EARLY RELIGIOUS TRAINING

The case data revealed another primary factor in the Christian experience of alcoholics. Eighteen of the twenty persons interviewed reported some degree of early religious training in their lives. This ranged from regular attendance at Sunday school and church to occasional church attendance and exposure to a strong religious model, such as a parent or grandparent.

Two persons who had no early religious training both had a restrictive Christian conversion. This indicates that a comprehensive conversion is more difficult for one who has not had some previous relationship with a Christian community. The dynamics of the experience, which interrupt deeply entrenched patterns of thought and behavior, are more likely to restrict his personal growth than to free him as a person.

Jean Piaget's study of the language and thought of children revealed that the verbal expressions of childhood serve functions other than communication. His analysis of these expressions give insight into the child's intellectual structure and orientation. He found that childhood speech falls into two categories: egocentric speech and socialized speech. The category of a child's verbal expressions indicates the developmental state of that child. He should progress from egocentric to socialized speech.[42]

Early religious training should help an individual to move from the level of egocentricity to the level of social concern. He learns that God cares not only for him but also for all people. He is rewarded for his kindness to others and receives kindness from others. The most important thing is that he is made aware of a supreme power which exists outside himself. His early training may have been a form of legalism which he has to reject. Even in rejecting this, he still retains the awareness of a higher power. The research indicates that this awareness returned to the alcoholic in his time of severe emotional stress. It gave him a point of reference to which he could turn. It gave him a ray of hope in his darkness. It served as the foundation for his own Christian experience. One man said, "When I turned to God, I made up my mind that I was going to be the kind of genuine Christian my grandfather was."

The outstanding example of the role of early religious training in the conversion of an alcoholic is the case of Mr. Taylor. This man had completely despaired, and hopelessness ruled in his alcoholism. He was living a life of immorality. He decided that his only hope was self-destruction. He bought a pistol and went out one night to the city dump, a location symbolic of his self-image. He fully intended to kill himself. As he walked around on that dump, he was torn in inner conflict. Suddenly, there appeared in his mind the image of a card with a picture of Jesus on it. Writen on the card was a verse, "Lord, be merciful to me a sinner." Mr. Taylor recognized the image as a card he was given in a Methodist Sunday school when he was a child. The verse became his prayer; he surrendered himself to

God; and he experienced a comprehensive Christian conversion. He is now a Methodist minister, working with alcoholics.

As in the life of Mr. Taylor, early religious training proved meaningful to the majority of alcoholics in this study. No matter how far they had drifted from that training, they were able to grasp it in the time when they needed it most.

VIII. THE ROLE OF THE HOLY SPIRIT

Each of the case histories gives evidence of the role of the Holy Spirit in the individual's experience. The alcoholics made no attempt to define or interpret the Holy Spirit. Neither is that the purpose of this section. The important point is that the individuals felt a definite sense of the spiritual presence of God, enabling them to break out of old patterns and into a new way of life. Wayne E. Oates points out that "the inspired responses of the developing self of Christians " is the best evidence for the integral presence of the Holy Spirit.[43] The responses of the alcoholics are the authorities in this matter.

Jonathan Edwards indicates that the Holy Spirit is the power, in conversion, which changes an individual's perception. He says that in those spiritual affections

> which are wrought in the minds of the saints, through the saving influences of the Spirit of God, there is a new inward perception or sensation of their minds, entirely different in its nature and kind, from anything that ever their minds were the subjects of before they were sanctified.[44]

The clinical research underscores Edwards' point of view. The recovered alcoholics spoke of how different the world seemed after their conversions. The persons who had appeared threatening before were seen as genuine friends afterward. A sense of isolation was transformed into a feeling of community relationship. One woman spoke of how wonderful it is now to get up in the morning, be inspired by the beauty of nature, and be able to look forward to a sober day. This woman expressed gratitude to God for her alcoholism. She said that through the struggle of this experience she had been taught a sensitivity to life which she had never known before. " The conflicts which men experience are ' teachable moments ' under the instructive tutelage of the Holy Spirit." [45]

Oates designates one function of the Holy Spirit in the life and work of a pastor as " the creative assimilation of new and strange experiences on the part of individual Christians and the fellowship of believers as a total community of faith." [46] The experiences studied in the research indicate that this function may be fulfilled in the individual's experience by the direct action of the Holy Spirit. Conversion is a strange and new experience. It is totally different from previous experiences. Awareness of the presence of the Holy Spirit enables the individual to interpret and assimilate his experience in the light of his spiritual needs and the reality of God. Under the continuing guidance of the Holy Spirit, the conversion experience may become an integrated and instructive part of one's total life. However, when spiritual pride interrupts the work of the Spirit, the conversion may assume gigantic proportions and become the consuming focus of one's existence. This is a restrictive consequence of spiritual pride, as indicated in Chapter II in the case of Mr. Wright.

Oates also refers to the role of the Holy Spirit as the power that activates " divine conviction from within." [47] Internal conviction is the only thing that will transform an alcoholic. No amount of cajoling by others, especially family members, will have any effect unless the individual is convinced from *within* that he needs help. The Holy Spirit is not bound to objective relationships. It enters the subjective regions of human experience and works within the internal frame of reference. The Holy Spirit is patient, but persistent. The individual is not deprived of his freedom of decision. He is, rather, enabled by the Holy Spirit to activate his decision-making ability.

Mr. Roberts is a converted alcoholic who attributes the " neurotic " depression of his years of drinking to the work of the Holy Spirit trying to awaken him to the reality of his self-destructive way of life. In his case, the role of the Holy Spirit served to intensify his feelings in an effort to raise the low point of his life and save him from destruction. Early religious training, vocational dissatisfaction, economic insecurity, and the loss of hope all became redemptive instruments of the Holy Spirit, working within the internal frames of reference and enabling this alcoholic to surrender.

IX. THE PROBLEM OF IDENTITY

Identity Diffusion. A common trait shared by the cases studied is a lack of a positive identity previous to their conversion. They exhibit unrest and dissatisfaction with their lives. One man had been involved in at least three vocations before his conversion. His personality development was arrested at adolescence. Life had no significant meaning to him. To use Horney's terms, such identity diffusion relates to the inner conflict between the actual self and the ideal self, and the absence of the real self — the locus of one's personal identity. This conflict is characterized by self-derogation.

Abraham H. Maslow points out that every self-defacing act is recorded in the unconscious.

> If we do something we are ashamed of it registers to our discredit, and if we do something honest or fine or good it registers to our credit. The net results ultimately are . . . either we respect and accept ourselves or we despise ourselves and feel contemptible, worthless, and unlovable.[48]

This characteristic of human nature is focused in the loss of self-respect observed in alcoholism. Each alcoholic interviewed reported a low self-esteem before his conversion. Eight reported they had lost absolutely all self-respect. The alcoholic knows that he has done wrong to himself and to others, and he despises himself for it. The self-derogation results in the chronic identity diffusion of alcoholics.

Erik Erikson places the developmental crisis of identity diffusion at the time of adolescence. Identity is achieved at various stages of development when there is a " successful alignment of the individual's *basic drives* with his *endowment* and his *opportunities.*" [49] Erikson defines ego identity as

> the accrued confidence that one's ability to maintain inner sameness and continuity . . . is matched by the sameness and continuity of one's meaning for others.[50]

Identity diffusion, then, is characterized by inner conflict and discontinuity between the way one sees himself and the way he is seen by others. Although Erikson centralizes the conflict in adolescence, he states that " identity *formation* neither begins nor ends with adolescence: it is a lifelong development largely unconscious to the individual and to his society." [51]

The alcoholic is unable to align his basic drives with his endowment or his opportunities. He experiences personal disharmony and social discontinuity. He is a person who has never learned who he is. Kierkegaard says that when something becomes possible and necessary, it becomes actual.[52] In the conversion experience the alcoholic has the chance to actualize his own identity. He sees himself as he really is. He is motivated to fulfill his potentialities as a human being. Possibility and necessity merge into self-identity. Identity formation in the conversion of the twenty alcoholics emerged in the form of religious, social, and vocational stability.

The Problem of Sexual Identity. The theory of the identity diffusion of the alcoholic is supported by a study of alcoholics and homosexuals by Robert J. Gibbins and Richard H. Walters. These men concluded that alcoholics have difficulty with sexual identity. However, the alcoholic does not necessarily identify with the wrong sex. He fails to identify firmly with either sex.[53]

There is evidence of this problem in the case of Mrs. Mills. This woman was the oldest of four girls in her family. She went to church regularly with her mother. Her father did not attend church. The mother did not drink, but the father drank alcoholic beverages outside of the home. The father was a barber and the mother worked as an office clerk. The father was the dominant parental figure in the family. He managed the discipline of the children, usually relying on verbal scolding for punishment. Mrs. Mills rates their marriage as average.

Mrs. Mills has made a strong identification with her father, to whom, she says, she felt closest. After she left home, she went through a period of time in which, like her father, she had no church relationship. Now she is a church member, but she attends only occasionally. She, like her father, began drinking in late adolescence. She was an alcoholic by the age of thirty. She identifies strikingly with her father's vocation. She is a hairdresser; he was a barber. She spoke of following his work as the natural thing for her to do.

Mrs. Mills has had a very difficult married life. Her first marriage ended in divorce. Her second marriage ended with her husband's suicide, and her third, and present, husband recently attempted suicide. All three men have been alcoholics. The case history indicates that Mrs. Mills's overidentification with her father, and lack of identification with her mother, created a problem of sexual identity. This has caused her to become involved in unhappy marital relationships. In spite of this, her Christian conversion and relationship with Alcoholics Anonymous is giving her a new source of personal and social identity that may compensate for her lack of clear sexual identity.

Negative Identity. The " despised self " attitude, which characterizes identity diffusion, may lead to what Erikson calls the " choice of a negative identity." [54] This is a perversely based identity in which the individual flatly and totally capitulates as a self to the negative characteristics with which he has been confronted. His appearance and behavior may reflect the negative attitude he has about himself. The alcoholic sees himself as worthless and is determined to prove it to everyone. This negative identity permits a person to steal, if necessary, in order to buy a drink; to beg; or to drink anything from cleaning fluid to fermented garbage.

Erikson says that some late adolescents — a chronic stage of development for the alcoholic — " if faced with continuing diffusion, would rather *be nobody or somebody bad, or indeed, dead — and this totally, and by free choice — than to be not-quite-somebody."* [55] Erikson's reference to death coincides with Karl Menninger's theory that alcohol addiction is a chronic suicide. In the interviews, the alcoholics frequently commented that there were many times in which they wished they were dead. When continuing identity diffusion and its related internal dangers threaten the individual, " alcoholism is chosen or substituted as a kind of lesser self-destruction serving to avert a greater self-destruction." [56] The irony of alcoholism is that " the self-destruction is accomplished . . . *by means of* the very device used by the sufferer to relieve his pain and avert this feared destruction." [57] The negative identity of the alcoholic blinds him to this otherwise obvious fact.

Christian conversion enables the alcoholic to find the basis of his identity. He is converted from a negative to a positive identity as a child of God. Upon this basis he can begin to find what his attributes are and what others can mean to him. He can move from a self-destructive to a constructive course in life. The development of a positive identity undergirds his sobriety and allows him to enjoy a full and free life. "Most conversion experiences," says Gardner Murphy, "reveal this process of self-discovery."[58]

X. THE PROBLEM OF MEANING

A lack of meaning pervades the life of a practicing alcoholic. A number of interviewees responded that before their conversion they did not care whether they lived or died. When the meaninglessness of their existence became more fearful than death, two of the persons planned to take their own lives. Death may be a welcomed escape from a meaningless life. Approximately 50 percent of traffic accidents involving death or injury are directly related to the consumption of alcohol.[59] This suggests that driving while intoxicated may be a subtle, unconscious way of choosing death over a meaningless life.

Zanie Ruth Adams, a public-health nurse, has called attention to the "empty cup" aspect of alcoholism.[60] Alcohol fills the emptiness of an individual's life. It is an effective way of making one's cup run over. It never fails to fill the empty cup, but neither does it fail to destroy personal freedom and integrity in the process. Alcohol offers only temporary release from the pain of meaninglessness. After it has been consumed, the "cup" is empty again.

Viktor E. Frankl has called this emptiness an "existential vacuum." This is characterized by "a loss of feeling that life is meaningful."[61] The individual who experiences this sense of meaninglessness seeks ways by which to deny the boredom of his existence. This often results in neurotic behavior other than alcoholism. A fanatical zeal about sports, work, religion, or almost any other part of one's life may indicate an "existential vacuum." Sexual perversion or promiscuity is also a consequence of this vacuum. Frankl sees this as a widespread phenomenon of the twentieth century. He says that "the struggle for existence is a struggle 'for' something; it is purposeful, and only in so being is it meaningful and able to bring meaning into life." [62]

The " existential vacuum " is a clear description of the alcoholic. He is searching for meaning. When he finds that alcohol provides only temporary relief, followed by deepened anguish, he is at the point of surrender. He is open to the possibility of Christian conversion. The alcoholic's " cup " remains empty unless, in conversion, he can find the higher spiritual values that he needs to fill it. In Christian conversion, the " existential vacuum " is filled with a new meaning and purpose in life. Research indicates that with something to live for, the alcoholic can recover and find useful outlets for his growing inner resources.

XI. The Problem of Harmony of Values and Behavior

Anton Boisen cites the case of a man named Rudolph who was born in Germany of respectable, middle-class parents. His father was very strict and his mother was very lenient. At the age of sixteen, Rudolph came to America. He was a well-meaning, conscientious boy. He had accepted the external standards of his parents and society, but he developed a serious problem. " He had not brought himself into harmony with the standards he had accepted." [63] Rudolph reached a state of anxiety over the adolescent problem of masturbation. It became a compulsion to him. At the point of mental collapse, he consulted a doctor, who advised him to try religion. Rudolph attended a revival meeting and experienced a religious conversion, which relieved his tension and changed his life.

Boisen's discussion of Rudolph reflects a difficulty that appeared also in the case studies. The alcoholic is often a person who experiences disharmony between his beliefs and his behavior. Whereas masturbation was Rudolph's compulsion, drinking is the compulsion of the alcoholic. Just as Rudolph knew that compulsive masturbation was wrong, the alcoholic knows that compulsive drinking is wrong. Both have in common the fact that in and of themselves, they have no control over their behavior. Surrender of the self with its old patterns of disharmony is the only thing that allows the formation of harmony between values and behavior.

The case of Mr. Kemp, which has already been discussed, illustrates this point. In his limited conversion experience, at a revival, Mr. Kemp accepted a standard of values that he fully believed to be right. These were the Christian values of his wife and, particularly, of his stepfather, whom he greatly admired. However, Mr. Kemp was unable, at that time, to surrender himself to those values. There was no internal commitment to his intellectual affirmations. His drinking, instead of improving, became more compulsive. For six years he lived a conflictual, anxiety-ridden existence. There was complete disharmony between his religious beliefs and his manner of living.

It was not until Mr. Kemp was able to surrender to his Christian values and experience a comprehensive conversion that his compulsion to drink subsided. He, like Rudolph, was able to effect harmony between his values and his behavior through the experience of comprehensive Christian conversion.

XII. THE ROLE OF FAMILY BACKGROUND AND PARENTAL ADEQUACY

The role of family background and parental adequacy was a significant factor in the dynamics of the cases studied. Eight persons rated their parents' marriage as happy; five rated them as unhappy; two rated them as average. Five reported their parents' marriage ended in divorce while they were still at home. Five did not rate their parents' marriage because they were not raised by both parents and could not evaluate this. Of these cases, two reported the death of the father in their early childhood; two reported the death of the mother in their early childhood; one reported the death of both parents in her early childhood. One man, who rated his parents' marriage as happy, stated that his father was completely and permanently paralyzed when the child was four years of age. This had the effect of depriving this person of a father at an early age.

Of the twenty cases studied, exactly half experienced the early deprivation of at least one parent either by divorce or death. Of the five women interviewed, three had lost their father in early childhood. One of these three lost both parents. In eight of the ten deprived cases, the lost parent was the father.

The degree of family instability in the sampling exemplifies how important this is for the alcoholic. He is often a person who has never known a stable, secure environment. He has either had weak models to learn from or has had no models at all. The importance of the father's role is strongly supported by the data. The absence of the father left a chasm in the lives of these persons which was never filled, except in the case of Mr. Kemp. His stepfather did become a meaningful person to him.

The use of alcohol in the family varied in the sampling. The outstanding fact in this regard is that eleven reported that the father drank and the mother did not. This suggests an ambiguity in the parental standards imposed upon the child, which created confusion and indecisiveness, and this possibly led to personal instability. Only two persons stated that both parents drank. Two persons stated that their father was an alcoholic, and one stated that both parents were alcoholics. This low percentage rules out the already disproven theory that alcoholism is hereditary.[64] Three persons reported that neither parent drank, and four were unable to give information.

The Christian conversions of these alcoholics attest to the vital function that religion has in the life of a parentally deprived person. A clear concept of the fatherly role of God fills the chasm left by death, defection, divorce, and all other relationship-breaking forces of life. In these cases, religion did not become a " substitute " for deprivation. It became a strengthening resource for making personal decisions, accepting responsibility, and maintaining a sober life.

CHAPTER IV

Christian Conversion
and Personality Theory

ALCOHOLISM and Christian conversion are experiences that vitally affect the total personality. Theories of personality provide a framework within which a holistic approach to the conversion of the alcoholic is possible. The theoretical models of personality that support this study are drawn from the writings of two men who have combined theoretical formulation with clinical practice — an American psychiatrist, András Angyal, and a Polish psychiatrist, Kazimierz Dabrowski. The clinical material is considered in the light of the theories of these men.

I. THE THEORY OF ANDRÁS ANGYAL

Angyal was concerned with both theory and therapy.[1] His theory is based on a holistic approach to personality. Angyal's basic tenet is

> that personality is an organized whole and not a mere aggregate of discrete parts. Its functioning does not derive from the functioning of its parts; rather the parts must be viewed in the light of the organizational principles governing the whole.[2]

Angyal focused upon the structure of personality and the basis of neurosis. His contributions give fresh understanding to the dynamics of alcoholism. His affiliation with the Yale Center of Alcohol Studies indicates his interest in this area of research.

Foundations of Angyal's Personality Theory

Angyal defines life as a "process of self-expansion." [3] The creativity of the organism allows it to move beyond its own limits. This process of self-expansion does not take place within the organism. It involves the interacting of the organism with the environment. Organism and environment are the two necessary ingredients of the process of life.

The Trend Toward Autonomy. The distinctive feature of living organisms is their autonomy. "Life is, to a large extent, a *self-governing* process." [4] When the total process of an organism is considered, there is "a definite trend in organismic total process toward an increase . . . of autonomy." [5] Each stage of development is characterized by an increased sense of autonomy. Angyal points out that although there is movement toward greater autonomy, the organism is not always successful in achieving it. He is thrown back at times by environmental influences with which he must interact.

The trend toward autonomy in the process of self-expansion is limited by outside influences and by the nature of the given organism. Whenever the organism experiences regressive episodes, there is a reduction of autonomy. Regression may be of two types: "passive setback and strategic retreat." [6] The passive setback occurs when the organism is overwhelmed by heteronomous forces against which it is powerless. Strategic retreat occurs when "a situation becomes untenable at a complex level, and the person retreats to a more primitive and familiar one to gather his forces for a new advance." [7]

The alcoholic shows his autonomous strivings by his defense against outside interference with his drinking patterns. Angyal says that such a person will resent and resist any intrusion into his activities; he will oppose domination by others, assert his right to his property, protect his privacy, and in general resist any encroachment of his sphere of freedom and mastery.[8]

Any encroachment upon the alcoholic's right to drink is resented and resisted. He protects his supply of alcohol in secret places and guards it with his life.

Alcoholism is a disturbance of healthy autonomy through the distortion of *excessive* autonomy. Alcohol becomes the battleground upon which a person stakes his life. The alcoholic uses alcohol to compensate for real or felt inadequacies. It is a reaction to threat. It gives him a false sense of autonomy, which, in reality, undermines his trend toward true autonomy.

The Trend Toward Homonomy. Angyal points out that " human behavior cannot be understood solely as a manifestation of the trend toward increased autonomy." [9] Even as the individual has a strong need to maintain his autonomous self, he has a need to " surrender himself and to become an organic part of something that he conceives as greater than himself." [10] It is evident that " the trend toward homonomy, the wish to be in harmony with a unit one regards as extending beyond his individual self, is a powerful motivating source of behavior." [11]

The alcoholic, with his excessive autonomy, resists this trend in himself. He denies his need for God or others. He walls off durable relationships and projects an image of self-sufficiency. Only when his false autonomy is shattered does he surrender to the human trend toward homonomy. His personal impoverishment and spiritual bankruptcy, when confessed, motivate him toward healing relationships. The superficial " drinking buddy " relationships of the past must be superseded by meaningful, sober encounters with persons and the formation of faithfulness.

Alcoholism is a form of " overcommitment," which

Angyal says is a basic disruption of the trend toward homonomy. The individual overcommits himself to alcohol and
all other relationships are cast aside. "This overcommitment leads inevitably to resentment." [12] Resentment breaks
relationships and isolates persons. The individual then re-
turns to his false, alcoholic autonomy to escape the fear of
isolation. The case histories show that conversion disrupts
this cycle of reaction and enables the individual to form new
and healthy patterns of behavior.

The Concept of the Biosphere. Angyal places the two
trends of human personality within a concept called "the
biosphere." He says that "in the biosphere two definite directions can be distinguished: autonomous determination or
organismic government and heteronomous determination or
environmental government." [13]

These trends move in opposite directions, yet they are
"united in the total dynamics of the biosphere." [14] There is
tension between the biospheric poles of self-determination
and self-surrender. In the healthily functioning personality,
these two orientations are complementary rather than con-
flicting. For example, Angyal points out that to enter a loving relationship requires not only self-surrender but also a
degree of resourcefulness and self-reliance. To put it in
existential terms, one must belong if one is to be, and one
must be if one is to belong.

Bionegativity. A healthy personality has all its trends and
part processes well integrated, each promoting the total
functioning of the personality. Angyal refers to the opposite
of biospheric harmony as "bionegativity," which "may be
defined as a personality constellation in which one or more
part processes disturb the total function of the organism." [15]
Bionegativity is a relational term. It does not refer to the
personality as such, but rather to the disruption of the part
processes functioning within the personality.

Alcoholism demonstrates how bionegative disturbance is
a chain reaction phenomenon. One disruption sets off
others. The alcoholic, who may have formerly been a highly

moral person, often is found lying, cheating, and stealing. Alcohol addiction disrupts the basic personality integration and leads to further breakdown of other aspects of the personality.

The Case of Mr. Wolf. The case of this middle-class businessman illustrates the basic validity of Angyal's personality theory. Mr. Wolf showed an early, rebellious trend toward autonomy by beginning to drink at the age of fourteen. Alcohol was not used by either parent. They were members of a Baptist church and attended regularly. Mr. Wolf was close to his mother but had little respect for his father. He had become a heavy drinker by the age of twenty-one. His alcoholism soon followed. During these years he was totally detached from the church, another indication of autonomy in the face of his parents.

Mr. Wolf married, but his alcoholism caused serious marital conflict. His best friends would have nothing to do with him. Excessive autonomy is indicated by his visiting prostitutes and his general immoral behavior. Mr. Wolf gave up all homonomous relationships in projecting his false, alcoholic autonomy. He said: "My wife hated me, and my children couldn't stand the sight of me. One son would leave the house whenever I came home and the other would miss supper just to keep from having to sit across the table from me." He could not maintain a loving relationship because he denied the trend toward homonomy, his own need for self-surrender. The conditions of his life had become "bionegative." The part process of alcoholism dominated and disturbed the total functioning of his personality.

Finally, in despair and isolation, Mr. Wolf did surrender and become sober. His Christian conversion opened the doors of a new life for him. He was helped by Alcoholics Anonymous, and his homonomous needs began to develop. However, his strong autonomous striving continued to operate. He remained in Alcoholics Anonymous for only three months. He does not attend at all now. He ceased to enjoy the meetings after he became secure in his sobriety. He joined and became active in a Methodist church. This was another autonomous act, but one that shows the acceptance of his need for homonomous relationships. His family relationships are meaningful now. Mr. Wolf found his true autonomy through self-surrender. Now these trends are balanced, although he has to take care not to let his strong autonomous needs dominate his interpersonal relationships. If this happened, his detachment and isolation could recur.

Personality as a Time Gestalt

Angyal views life as a series of occurrences. The past is never a closed book. It is always related to the present and to the future. He refers to personality as a " time Gestalt." [16] By this he means that personality

> exists not only at a given moment, that the person is not only what he is here and now, but that he is an organized process extending through time.[17]

Angyal states that there is definitely a sense in which the past cannot be changed. What is done cannot be undone. However, viewing personality as a time Gestalt, " past occurrences gain new ' positional values,' new significance in the changing personality." [18] Although past behavior cannot be changed, the *meaning* of past behavior can be changed.

The case of Mrs. Ross demonstrates the meaning of the past. Mrs. Ross says that she would rather die than relive her past. Her alcoholism was a terrifying nightmare. Yet, she is grateful for the past. Alcoholism, she says is her gift from God. Having experienced and having been delivered from it, she now has deep sensitivity toward life and confidence in life. The past has gained new " positional value " in her life since her conversion. Its meaning has changed with her personality.

Dimensions of Personality. Angyal suggests that one's life course is lived in three dimensions. The first is the dimension of *progression*. This is one's history of personal achievement. It is marked by hesitancy and changes. The dimension of progression is conditioned by the quality of commitment an individual puts into his goals and purposes.

The second dimension is *depth*. In this dimension the person " grows toward an increased anchoring of the self in a system of values giving meaning to his life and toward greater facility and perfection in expressing these values in actual behavior." [19] This involves self-discovery and self-expression. A simultaneous dimension is *breadth,* the aspect of life that enables an individual to express his basic needs through acceptable channels. Failure to develop breadth often results in the formation of narrowness and rigidity in the personality. " The fullness of life depends upon the harmonious growth of the personality structure in all three dimensions." [20]

The personality of the alcoholic has been interrupted at all three dimensions of life. His life course becomes regressive rather than progressive; his standard of values is dissolved and life's meaning is destroyed. He develops a narrow, restrictive outlook on life, withdrawing from the dimension of breadth. Research indicates that the healthy conversion process restores these dimensions to an individual's personality and allows him to progress and increase the depth and breadth of his life course.

Personality Disequilibrium. Evolution of a Gestalt " takes place in successive stages of differentiation and of re-embedding of the differentiated parts into the whole." [21] Differentiation, the discerning of individual parts, involves disequilibrium of the personality. It moves beyond the status of the whole. The part gains an individualistic character, and connection between the part and the whole becomes looser.

In the process of reembedding, the part loses this character " and again becomes integrated into the whole which may itself be enriched and changed in the process." [22]

Alcoholism presents a picture of disequilibrium. Differentiation has taken place, but it has become a chronic state. The total personality remains loosely connected and under the influence of the alcoholic compulsions within the personality. Conversion is a kind of shock treatment that activates the fixated disequilibrium and allows reembedding to take place. When this happens, the total personality has been enhanced in the process. Case after case reveals that the life of a converted alcoholic may be happier and more productive than was his life prior to alcoholism.

Decision and Risks. Angyal recognizes that it is necessary for anyone to take reasonable risks. The alternative is an inactive, uncreative life. " One never can be entirely certain of the later effects of any steps one takes in life." [23] Any human decision requires calculation of risk.

> Every decision or choice narrows down the possibilities of the future. . . . What a person does at any time commits him to a future course to be taken, sometimes far beyond any realistic necessity.[24]

The decision to drink involves the risk of alcoholism. The longer a person drinks, the greater commitment he makes toward alcohol addiction. He narrows down the possibilities of his future. What began as a decision may become a compulsion, which has nothing to do with decision. The drinker never knows what will be the future consequences of his drinking. As a time Gestalt, the alcoholic's personality in the present is always related to his past. This may explain why so many recovered alcoholics devote their lives to helping other alcoholics. They cannot extract themselves from their past. They can only change the meaning of the past and use it for the benefit of others.

Angyal's Concept of Neurosis Applied to Alcoholism

Angyal says that a theory is useful in that it operates

> as a guide, as a point of reference, for empirical studies, which otherwise are likely to result in an . . . in-

coherent mass of data. The utility of a good theory is twofold: it allows us to question nature intelligently and offers a background for the interpretation of empirical data.[25]

He applies his theory to the nature of neurosis, but it also serves as a useful framework for a clinical study of alcoholism.

The Organization of Alcoholism. With his emphasis upon the interrelation of the parts of the personality, Angyal states that

> neurosis is not a partial disturbance limited to just one province of personality. Neurosis is a sweeping condition. It is, in fact, a way of life — self-destructive to be sure, but nonetheless a way of life.[26]

The total life is organized around the neurosis and controlled by it.

> The strength of a neurosis is due precisely to the fact that it is not a mere collection of separate items but an organization with its own vitality, which is sustained and perpetuated by the principles of system action and cannot be obliterated or dislodged by any segmental partial changes.[27]

Alcoholism, like neurosis, is an organization. The alcoholics in the sampling spoke of their drinking as a "way of life." Family, friends, job, church, and all other aspects of their lives took a secondary role. Life became carefully organized around alcohol. Alcoholism gains its strength through its self-perpetuating force. The promise to stop drinking is not enough to disrupt this organization. This represents a segmental change which cannot displace the powerful alcoholic patterns. Only total surrender, as evidenced in the case histories, will overthrow the alcoholic organization.

Anxiety and Isolation. Angyal states that practically all

theories agree that the crucial and basic issue in psycho-
pathology is anxiety. " It is anxiety that creates, or marks,
the parting of the ways between health and neurosis." [28]
Anxiety may be conscious or unconscious. However, " overt
anxiety occurs in only a small fraction of neurotic conditions. In a chronic obsessive-compulsive neurosis, e.g., it is
very hard to detect any conscious anxiety." [29] In a chronic
obsessive-compulsive state, the alcoholic may show relatively little overt anxiety. As long as his compulsive needs
are being met, he continues to function. However, he is
plagued by a " hurrying, rushed, driven feeling; a general
inner restlessness." [30]

The life situation that reveals anxiety most dramatically
is the " *state of isolation.*" [31] This state is characteristic, in
some degree, of each alcoholic in the sampling. Mrs. Simmons' neighbor characterized her as very withdrawn and
unfriendly during her alcoholism. He said that he lived
next door to her and hardly ever saw her. Mrs. Simmons'
conversion broke the bonds of isolation and allowed her
freedom from pathological anxiety.

Fear and Fantasy. Angyal gives two characteristics of
neurosis as *fear* and *fantasy.* Neurotic fear is indicated by
an " *overemphasis on security.*" [32] The alcoholic spends a
major part of his time and energy defending and protecting
himself. When the world becomes too threatening, the alcoholic hides in the stupor of intoxication, his " suit of
armor." Behind the facade of anger and resentment lurks
the feeling of fear. His " *compulsivity* " indicates the degree of his fear, and his fear of failure predetermines an
" *absence of real fulfillment.*" [33] The alcoholic does not
drink because he enjoys it. He drinks to prove that something will dispel his fear. Because this fails to work and the
fear remains, his life is " *not lived in the present.*" [34] He
plans to stop drinking *tomorrow,* and things will improve.
In an effort to escape the dangers of today, he projects himself into tomorrow.

The alcoholic lives in " *a world of fantasy,* a world populated with nonexisting figures, ghosts of an ill-perceived past." [35] This is particularly evident in the alcoholic phenomenon of delirium tremens. The alcoholic has distorted images of people, situations, and himself. This distorted perception increases his fear and strengthens his compulsion to drink.

The Theory of Universal Ambiguity

Angyal's central theory regarding the nature of neurosis is the "theory of universal ambiguity." He derived this from his concept that

> man is to be understood not in terms of any specific traits he possesses, or any specific patterns they form, but in terms of the overall pattern that organizes these traits and their multiple interconnections. [36]

Broadly speaking, personality is a dualistic organization. It includes two unalterable trends, autonomy and homonomy. This dual orientation operates in health or in neurosis.

The theory of universal ambiguity means that everything in life has a double meaning. The dual organization of personality is referred to as an

> ambiguous Gestalt, each part process having a different function and meaning, depending on whether it takes place within the Gestalt of health or the Gestalt of neurosis. [37]

Neurosis is not a part of the personality. It *becomes* the personality. Likewise, health is not buried in a dark corner of man's existence. " Health is present potentially in its full power in the most destructive, most baneful, most shameful behavior." [38]

The same process that creates neurosis contains the dynamics for creating health. This is the ambiguity of human life. Sickness of the personality takes place within the individual, within his personality organization. It is not brought in from outside his personality. Health, in like manner, grows within the person. Both patterns, health and neurosis, are coexistent in the same system, but only one can be seen at a time. This will be the dominant pattern. The coexistence of these two opposing organizations is manifested through a sudden shift in the expression of the personality. Angyal indicates that

> such dramatic, seemingly sudden shifts are rare, but they do happen. Foremost among them are the phenomena of conversion, such as religious conversions, . . . those described in some case histories of Alcoholics Anonymous, and the less well known, spontaneous radical changes which are not formulated by the person in religious terms.[39]

The clinical research revealed the existence of universal ambiguity in the experience of alcoholics. The coexistence of the patterns of health and sickness is evident in the rapid changes in personality manifestations. The emergence of the healthy personality, overthrowing its alcoholic counterpart, is not a " new " pattern. According to Angyal's theory, the potential health has been in the personality all the time. The case histories show that, through surrender and conversion, the potential health broke the bonds of alcoholism and assumed dominance in the personality. This accounts for the sudden feelings of peace and well-being which accompany conversion.

This theory works in reverse as well. When the healthy pattern becomes dominant, the potential alcoholic pattern continues to inhabit the personality. It becomes a real threat whenever the pattern of health begins to weaken. Alcoholics recognize the possibility of an outbreak of the alcoholic compulsion at any time. They guard against this by daily prayer and surrender. Conscious awareness of the unhealthy pattern enables them to remain healthy.

Several recovered alcoholics said they had never known anyone to return to alcoholism who consciously asked God for help in staying sober every morning and thanked Him

every night. They discounted the idea that anyone could
" slip " back into alcoholism. The recovered alcoholic who
resumes drinking does not " slip." He allows himself to forget the ambiguity of personality and the ever-present threat
of unhealthy patterns in a time of health. Angyal's theory
of universal ambiguity is an excellent framework for understanding the experience of the alcoholic.

The Pattern of Noncommitment

Angyal states that involved in almost any case of neurosis is " *the pattern of noncommitment.*" [40] This pattern is
characterized by a state of uncertainty in which an individual responds to significant persons with both love and
hostility. It causes him to search for a way to dispel confusion and gain a stable position in the world. The pattern of noncommitment is " the outcome of an abiding confusion as to whether the world is basically friendly or inimi-
cal." [41] The " noncommittal " person struggles " for a clear-
cut, reliable, unshakable attitude toward life, for guide-
posts and rules to live by." [42] In the process, he remains aloof
and detached.

Inconsistent Behavior. One factor that stands out in this
pattern is the inconsistent behavior of significant adults to
whom the person was related as a child. The case studies
showed this to be true of alcoholics in their parents' drinking
patterns. Eleven reported that their father drank but their
mother did not. This indicates that in over half of the cases
there was inconsistency in parental behavior. The confusion that this created in the mind of the child may have
been a central factor in the genesis of his later instability.
Angyal concludes that whether or not severe deprivations
and traumata are present in the case, " the confusion-foster-
ing factors are never missing." [43] Parental inconsistency,
apart from drinking patterns, was reported by Mrs. Dunn,
whose father was kind and open-minded and whose mother
was harsh and rigid. The resulting confusion led her into
a sequence of interpersonal failures.

State of Tension. The tension felt by the noncommittal person may not be noticed outwardly. However, inner tension is characteristic of this pattern. For example, many alcoholics are also chain smokers. This was evident in the interviews. At least one half of the respondents chain-smoked during the interview. Only three did not smoke. Heavy smoking was also observed at the Alcoholics Anonymous meetings that the author attended. Tension is often channeled through some acceptable act such as smoking. In the case of Mrs. Ross, tranquilizers became a means of reducing tension, secondary to alcohol, until her state of tension was relieved through Christian conversion.

The state of tension sometimes inhibits a person's speech. A number of the alcoholics interviewed said that during their active addiction they could not have talked with an " outsider " while sober. They could not have put a sentence together without long pauses, stammering, and confabulation. The author found this to be true in talking with practicing alcoholics.

The Self-image. A noncommittal person vacillates between considering himself to be worthless or to be of some value. " The all-important question is, ' Am I strong enough or too weak to cope with the hostile world? ' " [44] As previously stated, the clinical research showed the prevailing low self-esteem of alcoholics. This is intensified by frequent experiences of embarrassment and humiliation. His private answer to the above question is negative. Angyal states that " self-derogation in these people reaches an unbelievable degree." [45] This is similar to Erikson's " negative identity." [46]

The Hostile Orientation. The noncommittal person is more at ease with hostility than with love. The hostile orientation coincides with his low self-esteem. However, hostile aggression is usually inhibited and channeled through a neurotic pattern, such as rejecting responsibility or accepting it and refusing to follow it through. It may take the form of an obsessive-compulsive act such as masturbation, which " is always an expression of hostility and has only an indirect relation to sex." [47] This inhibition of hostility may be seen in a person's inability to look another person straight in the eyes.

The alcoholic has a hostile orientation toward the world. He thinks too little of himself to express it openly while sober. He keeps his hostility pent up until he is drunk. Then it gushes out, hurting everyone but himself. A counselee told the researcher that she could not understand how her husband could be so " sweet " when he was sober and so "mean " when he was drinking. This characteristic of alcoholism reflects the theory of universal ambiguity. Alcohol, in the process of depressing the healthy pattern, releases all the repressed hostility of the neurotic organization.

Seventy-five percent of criminal acts are directly related to the consumption of alcohol.[48] This figure demonstrates the role of alcohol in releasing hostile aggression, which, otherwise, may have been inhibited by the normal functioning of the healthy structure. One alcoholic, in the sampling, demonstrated his hostility dramatically by shooting at the minister who came to his home while he was drunk. Christian conversion has the effect of removing the inner core of hostility. Eight respondents reported that a primary feeling immediately after their conversion was love.

The Loving Orientation. The alcoholic, with his inhibited hostility, lacks a loving orientation. " In the pattern of noncommitment the impulse to love is most deeply hidden and most difficult for the patient to accept." [49] The expression of tenderness does not fit the hostile orientation. It would only weaken the tenuous hold the alcoholic has on life. This makes the alcoholic, perhaps, the most unlovable person imaginable. The spouses of alcoholics attest to this fact in Alanon meetings. One attractive woman with an upper-middle-class appearance said: " One morning my husband was drinking and I got so mad at him I could have killed him. I went in the bathroom, shut the door, and said the serenity prayer, but it didn't do a damn bit of good! " The hostile orientation of alcoholics provokes a hostile response from others.

Angyal points out that there is another orientation working in the life of the noncommittal person. The presence of guilt indicates that, within a hated world, there exists a beloved world. The same world and the same people evoke hostile and friendly responses from the alcoholic. Guilt is not a response one gives to the hating of an enemy. It is what a person feels when he expresses hate toward those he actually loves. The ambiguity of the hostile and loving orientations deepens the alcoholic's sense of guilt. " Guilt incurred through confusing friend and foe is what creates and maintains the patient's image of himself as perverted and morally worthless." [50]

The Process of Recovery

Angyal's therapy is aimed at weakening the dominant neurotic organization to such an extent that the healthy structure of the personality will arise to ascendancy. Therapy involves three major periods: the time when the neurotic pattern is dominant; the struggle for decision; and the ascendancy of the healthy pattern.[51] This process also describes the experience of the conversion of the alcoholic and his recovery.

Dominance of the Neurotic Pattern. In this first period, a preconversion state, the alcoholic gains a gradual recognition of his destructive way of life. This is a laborious process in which the resources of health begin slowly to break through the surface. Gradually, the healthy pattern gains in equal strength with the sick pattern. It is during this period that the alcoholic may seek help. He may go to Alcoholics Anonymous, to a doctor, or to a minister. He knows he has a problem, but he does not know what to do about it. At least two of the alcoholics in the sampling entered a rehabilitation center in this phase of their recovery.

The Struggle for Decision. This is the crucial stage of recovery. It is the point at which the individual either moves toward health or regresses into the security of his illness. The alcoholic " wavers between the two ways of life that claim his allegiance." [52] When surrender occurs, there is a shift of the dominance from the sick pattern to the healthy pattern. The alcoholic breaks out of his compulsive and self-destructive way of life. He gains a new perspective of life. The sampling reported that in this stage their feelings of hopelessness and despair were replaced by hope, peace, and freedom.

Ascendancy of the Healthy Pattern. With the overthrow of the alcoholic compulsion, the individual begins to grow as a person. He renews broken relationships. He affirms his faith in God. As his confidence grows, he gains mastery over the " difficult art of staying well." [53] On a self-rating scale, the majority of respondents indicated that they felt they had moved from the worst possible way of life to the best possible way of life.

The Process of Reidentification. In his shift toward health, the alcoholic must begin to identify with a life of health. He must gain a new self-definition that includes the constructive expression of " autonomous expansion " and " homonomous integration." [54] In this process, it is essential that the focal difficulty, alcohol addiction, be overcome. Since the person's total life has been built around this compulsion, his recovery depends on his ability to deny this neurotic urge. This requires constant awareness of the recurrence of the compulsion and the ability to overcome it at its inception.

Angyal says that another necessary characteristic of reidentification is " that the affirmation is made not about how one will *behave* but about what kind of person one will be." [55] He states that

> drawing on the reports of reformed alcoholics one finds that they differ from the short-lived conversions in that the habit was given up not merely because of its specific deleterious effects; a broader change of at-

titude has rendered the habit incompatible with the dominant system.[56]

The case histories of this study overwhelmingly attest to the accuracy of Angyal's statement. Through their own decision, the alcoholics found that drinking was inconsistent with their new self-identity. Therefore, sobriety became an integral part of their self-image as they moved into a healthy, free life. Comprehensive Christian conversion gave these people a new self-definition rooted in the reality of God and the strength to meet the demands of a new life.

II. THE THEORY OF KAZIMIERZ DABROWSKI

Like András Angyal, Kazimierz Dabrowski is involved in therapy as well as theory.[57] Dabrowski refers to his concept of personality development, paradoxically, as the "theory of positive disintegration." Disintegration refers to disruption within the individual's personality and disharmony in his relationship to the external environment. This is a concept similar to Angyal's "bionegativity," discussed earlier in this chapter.

The basis of Dabrowski's developmental theory is his postulate that man has a tendency to evolve from lower to higher levels of personality. The progressive evolution of personality is not possible without disintegration of the personality. Dabrowski's primary contribution to the understanding of alcoholism and conversion is his view

that personality develops through the loosening of its cohesiveness — an indispensable condition of human existence. The developmental instinct, therefore, by destroying the existing structure of personality allows the possibility of reconstruction at a higher level.[58]

In the process of positive disintegration there are three essential phases:

1. The endeavor to break off the existing . . . structure which the individual sees as . . . restricting the possibility of his full growth and development.
2. The disruption of the existing structure of personality. . . .
3. . . . unification of the personality on a new and different level than the previously existing one.[59]

Personality develops through disruption of the existing restrictive structure, a period of disintegration, followed by a new, or secondary, integration. The loss of psychic unity of the individual, which is destroyed in disintegration, activates the developmental instinct. This contributes to reconstruction of the personality at a higher level. This theory is very similar to Anton Boisen's concept of personal stress. Positive disintegration may be likened to religious conversion. Negative disintegration may be likened to mental disorder.[60]

Disintegration of Personality

Dabrowski considers disintegration as a generally positive developmental process. Whatever negative aspect it has is minimized when evolutionary progress takes place. The process of disintegration,

> through loosening and even fragmenting the internal psychic environment, through conflicts within the internal environment and with the external environment, is the ground for the birth and development of a higher psychic structure.[61]

The old patterns are broken down and new patterns are given freedom to develop. Disintegration is a prerequisite for the " new birth " of religious conversion.

> Disintegration may be classified as unilevel, multilevel, or pathological; and it may be described as partial or global, permanent or temporary, and positive or negative.[62]

Unilevel Disintegration. Unilevel disintegration occurs in developmental crises, normal periods of stress, or in psychopathological conditions. It may be accompanied by nervousness or neurotic behavior. Rather than being a complex emotional disorganization, it consists of processes on a single emotional level. Unilevel disintegration is often a chronic stage in which destructive processes prevail over constructive ones. It is characterized by instability and ambiguity of thought and feeling. " Prolongation of unilevel disintegration often leads to reintegration on a lower level, to suicidal tendencies, or to psychosis." [63] It is like Angyal's first stage of therapy, when dominance of the neurotic pattern remains.

Multilevel Disintegration. Multilevel disintegration is a complication of the unilevel process. Additional emotional levels are involved. A total fragmentation of the existing internal environment exceeds that of unilevel disintegration. It is an acute process that is based

> on the psychic structure of the individual and on the arousal of shame, discontent, and a feeling of guilt in relation to the personality ideal.[64]

Multilevel disintegration is depicted by the appearance of sublimation, the redirection of an unconscious drive into new, appropriate channels of expression. This marks the beginning of secondary integration at a higher level of personality development.

Pathological Disintegration. Pathological disintegration occurs when evolutionary instinct is blocked and the positive tendency of disintegration is not allowed to develop. It features a chronic lack of identity, retardation of progressive development, and a constricting of the personality. It is similar to restrictive Christian conversion, described in Chapter II.

Partial and Global Disintegration. Partial disintegration involves only one part of the total personality. It is similar to a limited Christian conversion. An individual may intellectually affirm a creed, a doctrine, or a way of life, but he does not make a total commitment to his intellectual affirmations. Global disintegration, on the other hand, is a total experience that shocks and disturbs the entire personality. The personality is changed in the process.[65] Global disintegration clears the way for comprehensive Christian conversion.

Permanent and Temporary Disintegration. Permanent disintegration occurs in severe, chronic diseases, which have physical as well as mental complications. The alcoholic who has experienced chronic brain damage would fall into this classification. It allows for only limited religious experiences. Temporary disintegration is an acute process that " occurs in passing periods of mental and somatic disequilibrium." [66] It generally has a positive effect on the personality.

Positive and Negative Disintegration. Positive disintegration allows for full expression of the developmental instinct. Dabrowski describes it as enriching life, enlarging the horizon, and bringing forth creativity. Negative disintegration is at the opposite pole. Either it fails to promote personality development or it causes involution, a period of personality decline. The prevalence of symptoms of multilevel disintegration over unilevel ones, the predominance of global forms over partial ones, and the presence of self-control and creative tendencies give evidence that the process of disintegration is positive rather than negative.[67]

Secondary Integration. Secondary integration is the new personality organization that arises out of the disturbance of personality at lower levels of development. " The seeds for integration are the feeling of dissatisfaction, discouragement, protest, and lack of higher values and needs for them." [68] There is a definite and visible increase in the person's sensitivity to himself and to his environment. There is progressive movement to a richer, higher level of personality manifestation. Dabrowski suggests that secondary integration can become one of several forms. It can be:

1. A return to the earlier integration in more nearly perfect form; . . .
2. A new form of integration, but with the same primitive structure without a higher hierarchy of aims; . . .
3. A new structural form with a new hierarchy of aims.[69]

Development of the personality is indicated by the last form of secondary integration.

The Case of Mr. Booth

The case of Mr. Booth exemplifies the theory of positive disintegration. Mr. Booth's parents were divorced when he was five years old. He was shifted around from place to place during his childhood. He spent the longest period of time living with an aunt and uncle who were " religious fanatics." The uncle was also a " bootlegger," selling " moonshine " whiskey.

Mr. Booth began working in a drugstore when he was fourteen. He worked his way up to acting manager. Regular drinking began in his late adolescence. He was drafted into the army, where he, again, was given major responsibility. He showed early signs of being an ambition-ridden person. After his army experience, Mr. Booth returned home. His drinking continued for about ten years with no signs of compulsion.

The beginning of compulsive drinking coincided with indications of personality disintegration. Mr. Booth was hospitalized and operated on for a ruptured ulcer. He experienced emotional shock and fear. Having thought of himself as a self-sufficient, totally healthy person, he refused to accept this puncture in his ideal self-image. Defying medical advice, he got drunk the first time he was out of the house. He developed a negative, bitter, resentful attitude. He became dissatisfied and discouraged. He changed jobs and the tension lessened temporarily, but he continued his compulsive drinking. A second ruptured ulcer forced him to quit work. He experienced marital conflict as a result of irresponsibility toward his family. He took and lost other jobs, and his life became marked by total disintegration. His wife left him for six months. He hit bottom. He had lost his family, his job, and his self-respect.

One day Mr. Booth's complete personality disintegration began to take on a positive aspect. He became aware of the irrationality of his behavior. This awareness, although obvious to others, came as a shock to him. He felt the absence of higher values in his life and a need for them. He called the Alcoholics Anonymous office and went to a meeting that night. The lack of " phoniness " in the persons at the meeting confronted him with his own spiritual bankruptcy. He finally surrendered to God and accepted his help in becoming a new person. He experienced real inner struggle to stay sober for the first three months, but after that he had no trouble in living a sober, constructive life.

Mr. Booth experienced a multilevel, global disintegration. There was a total fragmentation of his internal and external environment. He felt shame, discontent, and guilt. The negative aspects of his disintegration were temporary and, therefore, marginal. His family returned and he now has a stable job. The positive development of his experience is identified by the development of a secondary integration at a higher level of functioning than he had ever manifested. He developed " a new structural form with a new hierarchy of aims." [70]

The comprehensive Christian conversion of Mr. Booth demonstrates that there is religious value to positive personality disintegration. Mr. Booth attributes his secondary integration to the grace and power of God. As stated in Chapter II, the work of the Holy Spirit can utilize the self-destructive, disintegrating force of alcoholism to redeem the individual and enable him to reintegrate at a higher level of personality development.

The Principal Dynamics of Multilevel Disintegration

Dabrowski's theory is composed of a number of dynamics. The principal ones include "the feeling of disquietude, shame, discontentment with oneself, guilt, inferiority feelings toward oneself, and 'subject-object' attitude." [71]

Disquietude. Disquietude arises from the attitude of the individual toward his own development. It is manifested in restlessness when the person becomes aware of his irresponsibility and inappropriateness of behavior. Disquietude symbolizes the development of sensitivity. It is the growth of feeling. Dabrowski says that this new awareness is a signal that the person is not living to his full capacity. He has potential at a higher level of functioning. Mr. Booth shows disquietude in his awareness of his irresponsible and inappropriate behavior. It motivated him toward a new way of life.

Shame. The growth of this strong emotion shows the person's sensitivity to the reactions of others. It shows that he cares about what they think about him. Dabrowski sees shame as "one of the first stages of loosening and disintegration of primitive structure and instinct in the process of multilevel disintegration." [72] Chapter II discussed the role of shame in the conversion experiences of alcoholics.

Discontent with Oneself. The feeling of discontent reflects the progress of multilevel disintegration. It is a symptom of healthy disapproval of one's inappropriate behavior. "It is an evidence of the birth and development of what is 'self' and what is 'not self' in the internal environment." [73] Self-discontent activates the developmental instinct to strive for higher levels of personality growth.

Guilt. Guilt involves disquietude, shame, and self-discontent. It is a powerful feeling that penetrates the personality and may demand expiation through compulsive activity. Alcoholism may be a kind of self-punishment derived from a deep sense of guilt. Dabrowski associates guilt with a person who has strong capabilities to function at a higher level but who chooses to remain at a lower level of development.

At least one case in the sampling illustrates this causation of guilt. Mr. Moorehead, who had been a " skid row " alcoholic, felt that most alcoholics are men and women of high potential who have not found any way to express and fulfill their potential. In his youth, Mr. Moorehead had been interested in intellectual and academic things. He spent much time in the city library. However, these interests were lost in the process of alcoholism. He had not found acceptable, rewarding channels for his intellectual quests. He ended up in a rescue mission, where he began a gradual experience of conversion. This man's present intellectual ability and his literary interests indicate a high degree of intelligence, which has found meaningful channels of expression since his conversion and sobriety. As an alcoholic, he had experienced a deep sense of guilt over the unfulfillment of his potential.

> The sense of guilt is an indispensable factor in the development and particularly springs forth in the individuals during rapid development. It contributes to the creative tension which forms the basis of self-education.[74]

Subject-Object Process. A normal aspect of positive disintegration is the creation of two opposing self-structures within the personality. This is the ability of an individual to see himself objectively. It is the attitude of retrospection. The person sees aspects of himself as though he were considering a self outside his own personality. Alcoholics reflect this process when, after a drunken bout, they say: " That wasn't really me doing that," or " I can't believe I did that." It is detachment from a self the person does not want to claim.

The Feeling of Inferiority Toward Oneself. Dabrowski differentiates between the problem of inferiority feelings toward one's environment, as described by Alfred Adler,[75] and the feelings of inferiority toward oneself. This latter feeling requires the development of a standard of values by which a person can measure himself. The case histories revealed that both social-class values and religious values played this role in the lives of the alcoholics. Also required is the development of the "subject-object process." It is the feeling that a person is inferior to his potential. He is not what he could be. This feeling occurs in individuals who are capable of development. In alcoholism, it would appear as a sign of positive disintegration.

> The feeling of inferiority toward oneself is one expression of the process of multilevel disintegration, and it arises from the greater self-awareness and the self-examination that occur in multilevel disintegration.[76]

The "Third Factor" in Personality Development

In addition to the influence of an individual's internal and external environments, Dabrowski includes a "third factor" in personality development. This "determines the direction, degree, and distance of man's development." [77] Dabrowski uses this factor to conceptualize the developmental instinct in man. Its appearance and growth are dependent, to some degree, on innate ability and environmental influences, but the "third factor" achieves a distinctive position in the personality. Its significance increases in the higher stages of human development. It is a necessary part of the maturation process.

Dabrowski describes this agent of personality development as

> a sort of active conscience of the budding individual, determining what represents a greater or smaller value in self-education, what is "higher" or "lower," what does or does not agree with the personality ideal, and what should be the course of internal development.[78]

The "third factor" appears in unilevel distintegration in an underdeveloped form, but it develops fully in multilevel disintegration. As a judging, deciding, and confirming agent in personality, it becomes an integral part of multilevel disintegration. It is a hidden, but present, factor that enables an individual to experience *positive* disintegration. As the personality gains stability in a secondary integration, the " third factor " is assimilated into the total personality and loses its effect as a separate function. Its work is seen in a time of developmental crisis.

Dabrowski suggests that each individual must acquire a " personality ideal," a dynamic goal toward which he directs his developmental energies.[79] The " third factor " motivates the individual toward his goal. It " strives to see that every concrete act of a given individual is in correlation with his personality ideal." [80] It enables the individual to weather the storm of disintegration and to receive positive benefit from severe stress. In directing the personality toward creativity and self-realization, the " third factor " ensures the personality's ability to master its impulses and compulsions. It is the energizing force of positive selfhood.

The development of this third agent alters, slowly but significantly, the individual's attitude toward his environment and toward himself. His relationship to his environment becomes clear and conscious. In becoming sensitive to higher values, the individual gains a sense of independency in his ability to choose his values. He learns to identify with groups that are congruent with his own self-consciousness and that help him to attain higher values in his life.

The person's attitude toward himself changes as the third agent allows for " self-education." This is " the process of working out the personality of one's inner self." [81] It involves a person's increasing self-awareness and ability to move toward a personality ideal.

The case of Mr. Grant illustrates the work of the " third factor." Having passed through the critical phase of alcoholism and having become identified with Alcoholics Anonymous, Mr. Grant gained an acute sensitivity to higher spiritual values. He developed a personality ideal toward which he directed his life. The development of a "third factor" in his personality enabled him to gain positive results from his experience of disintegration. He became identified with a group that coincided with his self-consciousness. He incorporated into his life higher spiritual values and a deepened relationship with God.

Theologically, Dabrowski's concept of the "third factor" may be interpreted in terms of the work of the Holy Spirit. It is no less nebulous than is an understanding of the Holy Spirit. It is significant that in this concept Dabrowski gives a clinical psychiatric observation which underscores a theological view of the work of the Holy Spirit. Like the Holy Spirit, the "third factor" is neither inherited nor imposed. It develops within the internal frame of reference. Its work appears in a time of personal stress. It motivates, rather than dominates, the personality. It allows the individual to assimilate his crisis experience into his total life process and convinces him from within of his need to change. Like the Holy Spirit, the "third factor" is not a permanent, separate force. It becomes an assimilated agent in the formation of clear, positive selfhood. The self becomes its own directing center. The concept of the "third factor" may be thought of as analogous to a doctrine of the Holy Spirit. The concept, however, should not be equated with the doctrine.

Kazimierz Dabrowski suggests a theory of personality that points out the positive role that seemingly negative feelings can have in personality development. His theory, like András Angyal's, serves as a frame of reference to increase one's understanding of the disintegration and conversion processes in alcoholism.

CHAPTER V

Christian Community and Recovery
from Alcoholism

THE PRECEDING chapters have examined the dynamics of Christian experience in alcoholism. As the context of this study, the Protestant parish fellowship plays a role in this experience. This chapter draws on the living experiences of alcoholics to explore the nature of the role of the Christian community in the recovery from alcoholism.

I. THE WAY THE ALCOHOLIC PERCEIVES THE CHURCH

Each person in the sampling had some relationship to a parish fellowship. The degrees of relationships to these parishes ranged from marginal to nucleus. In the interviews, the respondents were asked whether the fellowship of the church had helped them to refrain from drinking. The responses were evenly divided. Ten persons answered positively and ten persons answered negatively. These responses are, however, open to interpretation. The individual answered this question on the basis of his perception of the fellowship of the church. Whereas one person may take the word "fellowship" literally, in terms of interpersonal relationships, another person may interpret the fellowship of the church in terms of what it represents, such as a promise to God or a place of service. Of the persons who responded positively, only three spoke in terms of interpersonal relationships. The remaining seven spoke either in terms of their promise to God not to drink, or in terms of their position of responsibility in the church. Of the persons who answered negatively, all ten responded in terms of interpersonal relations. This indicates that three of the twenty recovered alcoholics have found within the church meaningful, supportive relationships which strengthen their ability to maintain sobriety.

The responses of the interviewees suggest that the alcoholic perceives the church as a place where one can learn about God as he is revealed in Jesus Christ. In terms of spiritual guidance and nourishment, eighteen of the respondents have found help in the church. This has come through worship, Bible study, and related opportunities. Nine of these eighteen have found a place of service in the church that is meaningful to them and gives them status in the community. However, at least twelve find their supportive fellowship solely in Alcoholics Anonymous and not in the parish fellowship. They see the church as an institution of teaching and service. Only a minority see it as a continuing, supportive fellowship of caring persons.

Dr. Edmonds, a recovered alcoholic, is one of the few persons who sees the church as a teaching institution, a place of service, and a sustaining fellowship. He is active also in Alcoholics Anonymous. He is attempting to learn more about the Christian faith through his church. He finds a place of service in the choir. His response to the interview question on the fellowship of the church was positive. He does feel that the interpersonal relationships within the church strengthen his ability to maintain sobriety. Mr. Phelps represented those who attend church regularly and derive spiritual meaning from their participation in worship, but who find no place of service in the church and do not consider it a supportive fellowship. Mr. Phelps is very active in Alcoholics Anonymous and finds his intimate relationships in that organization.

Mr. Roberts indicated the ambiguity within the church concerning drinking. When asked whether the fellowship of the church helped him to stay sober, he replied, " No, you don't get much encouragement from the church along that line when nine out of ten of the members drink themselves." He says that several deacons in his church continue to offer him a drink, even though they know he is an alcoholic. " They don't understand," he says. His philosophy is to listen to his fellow church members when they talk about something they know, such as Jesus Christ, but to ignore them when they discuss something they do not understand, such as alcoholism.

Mrs. Pope, one of the women interviewed, pointed out that there is a " hush-hush " attitude toward alcoholism in her church. It is never discussed. She attends the worship service regularly and finds support and understanding in the pastor, but she says the fellowship of the church does not strengthen her ability to refrain from drinking. All twenty persons stated that they did not feel that the church members understood alcoholism. They indicated frustration in knowing how to communicate the needs of the alcoholic to their church. Their eager cooperation in this project demonstrates their desire to inform others on any aspect of alcoholism.

II. Social-Class Factors in the Role of the Parish Fellowship

The case histories demonstrate the role of social-class factors in the relationship between the church and the alcoholic. Arnold S. Linsky states that

> the precise nature of the position taken by the churches . . . and the sanctions that have been employed have varied widely with the social and cultural setting of the church as well as with doctrinal differences.[1]

In his limited study, Linsky found that religious attitudes do play a strong part in the churches' views toward alcoholism, even when social-class factors are controlled. The research in this project revealed the significance of the social-class setting. Three cases, particularly, point out the role of social-class standards of acceptance in the church's attitude toward the alcoholic member.

The Case of Mr. Cole. This lower-class male is a member of the same Baptist church that he joined at the age of ten. His alcoholism began early in his twenties. Except for a period of time overseas during World War II, Mr. Cole has lived in the same lower-class community and attended the same Baptist church. His participation in the church continued, even though his alcoholism was known. He even taught a Sunday school class. During a period of two years when his wife had left him and his drinking was at its worst, he was absent most of the time from church. Only occasionally, when he was sober, did he go to church. During this time he did nothing other than drink. He stayed at home, alone, except when he went out to buy something to drink. He was able to exist because friends from his church occasionally left food and money with him. Mr. Cole was delivered from this acute phase of his alcoholism through a limited Christian conversion. He was welcomed back into the fellowship of the church.

The most significant aspect of Mr. Cole's case is his continuing relationship to the church in spite of his alcoholism. (John Dollard says that excessive drinking is not the social stigma in the lower classes that it is in higher classes of society.[2] Productivity is not so important in the lower class as it is in the middle class.) Mr. Cole grew up in this church, and his friends there never deserted him. He was always welcomed back during his worst years of drinking. Feeling accepted by them, he did not lose his own sense of self-respect. He leaned on them for support and they supported him. If he was confronted with his irresponsible behavior, he did not hear the confrontation. He said, " They acted like nothing was wrong." All he heard was care and concern. The church became a crutch on which he could lean whenever he needed it.

Although there are positive aspects to the church's relationship to Mr. Cole, there are also negative aspects. His social class did not condone his alcoholism, but neither did it confront him with a clear standard of values that would make him fully aware of his behavior. Although he reached a " gutter " existence, he was not allowed to hit bottom in terms of loss of self-respect and isolation from his community. To use Dabrowski's theory, he had no standard of values that would enable him to develop inferiority feelings toward himself or the subject-object process. This prohibited him from experiencing the full benefit of multilevel disintegration.

It seems that in a lower-class church Mr. Cole was excused and tolerated. Because he found continued support in his alcoholism, he did not surrender completely his old patterns of behavior. A sense of pride remained. This lower-class church offered Mr. Cole support, but it did not hold him responsible for his behavior. Its support was more in the form of tolerance than acceptance. As a result, Mr. Cole continues to have serious problems with alcohol.

The Case of Mr. Morris. This recovered alcoholic is a member of a lower-middle-class Baptist church. He had held a high-paying position as an engineer. Before his alcoholism began its degenerative effects, Mr. Morris was an active member of his church. He taught a Sunday school class and was involved in other church activities. As alcoholism began to interfere with his whole life, his participation declined until he had no relationship to the church. He experienced the feeling of total rejection by his church. He was isolated from all the members. No one from the church, except the pastor, came to see him during his acute alcoholism. While he was in a hospital in another city, he did not receive even a card from the church. During his hospitalization, Mr. Morris experienced a comprehensive Christian conversion. When he returned home he became active in Alcoholics Anonymous. He returned to his church, but he still felt rejected. His difficulty with alcohol was not mentioned and his reception was cool and detached.

Having lost his former job, he took the job as janitor for his church for six months. This seemed to symbolize his image in the church. He is presently working in his former vocation of engineering. Some progress has been made in his acceptance by the church, but it is a slow and painful process. After two years of sobriety, he still did not feel welcomed by most of the members. They made no effort to understand what happened to him or how his life had changed. He feels that most church members see an alcoholic as a " moral degenerate." Mr. Morris confesses a sense of resentment toward the church for its attitude toward him, but he prays daily that he will overcome this feeling. He attends the church faithfully, including Sunday school, and he feels a deep need for his relationship to the church. He had found little opportunity to share his conversion experience with anyone in the church, including the pastor. He states that the fellowship of the church does not strengthen his sobriety. The grace of God is his strength. Alcoholics Anonymous provides meaningful relationships outside the church. He feels that such open acceptance, as seen in Alcoholics Anonymous, will be possible in the church " only if the church members would admit that they are not perfect and that they have sinned, too."

This case study underscores Dollard's findings that there is a strong taboo on drinking in the lower-middle class. " Lower-middle people value highly the traits of respectability which differentiate them from the Lower group." [3] When Mr. Morris ceased to be respectable, he was isolated from his lower-middle-class community. He is now having to work his way back into the community by proving that he has gained respectability. This reaction is consistent with

Linsky's finding that "those church groups most strongly opposed to social drinking are also least accepting and supportive of the alcoholic person." [4]

In his process of disintegration, Mr. Morris was confronted with a clearly defined standard of values. This enabled him to move through a positive disintegration and experience a comprehensive Christian conversion. The case history shows that the real failure of his church was not that it rejected him during his alcoholism. He could understand this. It was that it refused to accept him, as a brother, back into the community and rejoice with him in his new life in Christ. Social-class images of respectability were placed above the redemptive grace of the Christian faith.

The Case of Mrs. Simmons. Before her alcoholism, Mrs. Simmons was an active member of an Episcopal church that represented an upper-middle segment of society. It was well known in the church that she drank and that she was a divorcée. These facts did not seem to matter. She was fully accepted in the fellowship. When her excessive drinking turned into alcoholism, she continued to go to church and was not rejected. She was confronted by her pastor about her drinking, but she denied that it was a problem.

When Mrs. Simmons realized that her drinking had become a serious problem, she began to attend Alcoholics Anonymous meetings. Within a few months she experienced a profound Christian conversion and gained sobriety. She went to her pastor to tell him what had happened, but she found only rejection. He discounted Alcoholics Anonymous as a crutch and said that he placed very little faith in conversion experiences such as hers. The church members reacted to her in the same manner. When it was known that she was an alcoholic and active in Alcoholics Anonymous, she was cut off from the church. No one made any effort to understand her experience. She could not remain in the church in the face of this rejection. She moved her membership to another Episcopal church where she found an understanding pastor. She has experienced meaningful relationships in this new church, but very few in the church know that she is an alcoholic. This fellowship does strengthen her sobriety.

This case demonstrates a significant fact concerning upper-middle-class reactions to the use of alcohol. Dollard states that this class has a neutral attitude toward drinking.[5] The church indicated this by its acceptance of Mrs. Simmons even with her excessive drinking. However, rejection came when Mrs. Simmons identified herself with a group of alcoholics — Alcoholics Anonymous. This was an identification outside the framework of the church membership. It made Mrs. Simmons an outcast who had to seek a religious community elsewhere — where she could begin again. Drinking is acceptable in this class, but confessed alcoholism is not. This parish fellowship would accept deviant behavior, but, ironically, it would not accept the confessing sinner who had found redemption.

These three cases point out the importance of social-class factors in the relationship between the parish fellowship and the alcoholic. Social class is a conditioning influence on the relationship, but not a determining factor. Linsky's study is a guard against any assumption that makes social class determinative. He shows that religious attitudes toward alcoholism are fairly consistent even when social-class factors are controlled. These combined studies indicate the complexity of the problem. It is evident that many factors enter into the relationship and that no one factor is determinative.

III. THE NEED FOR COMMUNITY

András Angyal has pointed out the " trend toward homonomy " that is present in every individual.[6] This underscores man's innate need for community. His autonomous strivings are successful only when they are balanced by meaningful interpersonal relationships. Paul E. Johnson has written that what the person needs to fulfill his potentialities and heal his fragmentation is a primary group characterized by "intimate face-to-face association and co-operation." [7]

Isolation and Community. Each case history in the sampling demonstrated some degree of isolation suffered by the alcoholic. Mr. Booth reached a point at which he felt totally alone in the world. He said that the greatest terror he had ever experienced was the feeling that he was the only person living in the world. He became unaware of the presence of others. He felt that even God did not exist. He described the intensity of his feelings as being " in the depths of hell with no way out or no one to hear me cry." Mr. Booth hesitated at this point in the interview so that his tears could subside. It was the only place where tears were evident as this man recounted his experience.

Each case also signifies a deep need for community. A first response after the initiation of their conversion experience was to move out of isolation and into community. For example, Mrs. Dunn's first act after her sudden conversion was to call the Alcoholics Anonymous office and find out where she could attend a meeting that night. She felt an immediate need for community. When Mr. Grant found release from his isolation, he attended an Alcoholics Anonymous meeting consistently for a year. Herbert A. Raskin, a psychiatrist, attests to this need for community by saying that " through every stage of the development of the addiction the person we are dealing with is helpless to make an adequate adjustment by himself." [8] The alcoholic needs others if he is to recover from the isolating effects of his illness.

For fourteen of the cases, Alcoholics Anonymous became the redemptive community that met their needs. Eleven of these were able to move beyond the community of Alcoholics Anonymous and establish themselves in a parish fellowship. Only three have made the parish their primary group and

Alcoholics Anonymous a secondary group. The remaining eight persons give first loyalty to Alcoholics Anonymous. They indicate that they have found an open acceptance there that cannot be equaled in the church. Six of the twenty cases found their immediate homonomous needs met through a parish fellowship. Alcoholics Anonymous, for these six, was either absent or secondary.

The clinical research indicates that the alcoholic usually has difficulty in finding an accepting, understanding community in his parish fellowship. The parish fellowship becomes meaningful after the immediate needs of the alcoholic have been met. When asked if the church did anything for them that Alcoholics Anonymous did not do, the majority of recovered alcoholics in Alcoholics Anonymous replied negatively. The minority who answered positively said that the church either taught them about God or gave them a place of useful service. Only two spoke specifically of meaningful relationships in their church. Johnson states that " without a community a church is but a shell or facade of what may once have been a corporate life." [9] The research revealed the lack of an open, accepting community within most of the parishes represented. These churches failed to be the redemptive community of Jesus Christ at a time of personal struggle and longing for relationships.

Dietrich Bonhoeffer suggests that one reason isolated persons cannot find warm acceptance in the parish fellowship is that most Christians take their life in community for granted. They fail to perceive visible fellowship as a blessing. " It is true," says Bonhoeffer, " that what is an unspeakable gift of God for the lonely individual is easily disregarded and trodden under foot by those who have the gift every day." [10] Those already in community may become insensitive to the isolation of the alcoholic.

The Parish Fellowship and the Alcoholic. The clinical research has revealed that alcoholics feel a lack of understanding of alcoholism in the churches. It showed that, although each alcoholic expressed his confession, only one of the twenty confessed before the church congregation. In most of the cases, alcoholism was never discussed within the church. There was an underlying feeling that the members of the parish fellowship projected their own sin upon the alcoholic. Mr. Morris stated this explicitly by saying that the church needed to admit its own imperfection before it could receive the alcoholic.

The research points to the fact that the church must be willing to confess its own sin before it can expect the alcoholic to confess his sin. A person who is as aware of his imperfection as the alcoholic is can find no home in a community that thinks of itself as perfect. This open, honest willingness to talk about his own faults makes the alcoholic identify strongly with Alcoholics Anonymous. As Mr. Booth expressed it, there is no " phoniness " in a confessing, concerned community. It is an indictment of the Protestant community that alcoholics find more concern and fellowship in Alcoholics Anonymous than in the church. Perhaps the churches need to listen to the wise words of a sensitive writer, Kahlil Gibran:

> Oftentimes have I heard you speak of one who commits a wrong as though he were not one of you, but a stranger unto you and an intruder upon your world. But I say that even as the holy and the righteous cannot rise beyond the highest which is in each one of you, so the wicked and the weak cannot fall lower than the lowest which is in you also. And as a single leaf turns not yellow but with the silent knowledge of the whole tree, so the wrongdoer cannot do wrong without the hidden will of you all.[11]

The church that is willing to stand under its own judgment and openly confess its wrongs and limitations provides a point of identity to which the alcoholic can turn. He must be accepted, not as an intruder, but as a fellow pilgrim in need of community and redemption.

The research points out the influence that social-class factors have in the churches' attitudes toward the alcoholic. It is apparent that the church must be aware of these factors if it is to guard against their subtle influences. The parish fellowship does not help the alcoholic by tolerating his behavior and serving as a crutch on which he may lean. Neither does it help him by total rejection. Real acceptance of the alcoholic involves making him responsible for his own mistakes. This does not mean trying to make him feel guilty by exposing his mistakes. The sampling showed that the alcoholic already has a deep sense of guilt. A caring community can suffer *with* an alcoholic, but it cannot suffer *for* him. Neither can it become sober for him. The parish fellowship can be a redemptive community if it is sensitive to the moment in which the alcoholic surrenders and reaches out for acceptance and understanding. At this point he is generally not strong enough to make his own way into the fellowship. He needs the quiet encouragement of others. The parish fellowship becomes the body of Christ when it expresses the spirit of unconditional forgiveness and grace toward the alcoholic. This becomes possible when the church recognizes that it is a human community, with all the imperfections that this implies. A redeeming community is always a confessing community.

The Parish Fellowship and Alcoholics Anonymous. Howard J. Clinebell, Jr., has called Alcoholics Anonymous " our greatest resource." [12] This study underscores the importance of his statement. Fifteen of the twenty persons interviewed had been helped directly by Alcoholics Anonymous. Clinebell reports that because of Alcoholics Anonymous,

> 130,000 alcoholics, a high proportion of whom had been labeled " hopeless " by their families, friends, doctors, and clergymen, are today living constructive, happy lives without alcohol. [13]

One alcoholic told that her pastor and parish felt that there was a direct conflict between the church and Alcoholics Anonymous. This attitude appeared at several points in the research procedure. The alcoholics expressed disappointment that more clergymen do not attend Alcoholics Anonymous meetings. This negative attitude toward Alcoholics Anonymous reflects the lack of understanding prevalent in the churches. It indicates that churches, like individuals, are threatened by what they do not understand.

The alcoholics in the sampling expressed a need for a close, working relationship between the church and Alcoholics Anonymous. They maintained that Alcoholics Anonymous cannot do everything that needs to be done for the alcoholic. For example, Alcoholics Anonymous can demonstrate the need for religious experience and dependence upon God, but it cannot teach the person about God or even help him to gain a clear concept of God. The alcoholic needs the spiritual guidance and direction provided by the church. The parish fellowship can also offer a wider scope of community relationships than Alcoholics Anonymous provides.

The parish fellowship is mistaken if it thinks it can meet all the needs of the alcoholic. It is also mistaken if it thinks it can do nothing for the alcoholic. The work of the Holy Spirit is not limited to the organizational framework of a given church, nor is the church dead. The case histories reveal the Holy Spirit at work in the lives of those who were isolated from the structure of the church as well as of those within the church. However, as well meaning as a parish fellowship may be, it is limited by its lack of empirical experience with alcoholism. The member of Alcoholics Anonymous knows what the alcoholic is experiencing, because he has been there himself. He has a point of identification that the wider fellowship does not have. The parish can learn from Alcoholics Anonymous if it views it as an ally in human redemption rather than as a competitor. The case histories that revealed *the healthiest recoveries from alcoholism are those in which the person is affiliated with both a parish fellowship and Alcoholics Anonymous.*

IV. THE ROLE OF THE MINISTER

The research revealed that pastoral care played a minor part in the alcoholics' recoveries. Only five of the twenty cases reported specific help given to them by their pastor. The most common response was that the pastor did not know what to do with an alcoholic and, therefore, did nothing. Each person replied that he thought there were definite ministries a pastor could perform, but that he was limited in what he could do. The pastor could be of help to the family of the alcoholic. He could seek an understanding of the needs manifested by the alcoholic. He is limited by time, knowledge of alcoholism, and, in many cases, his role as minister. Alcoholics may reject a minister if they see him as a moral judge coming to convert them.[14]

The Function of the Minister. Three cases illustrate the varieties of ways in which ministers responded to alcoholics in their parishes. The case of Mrs. Simmons, previously cited, points out the negative response of a pastor. The pastor had previously confronted Mrs. Simmons regarding her excessive drinking. At that time, Mrs. Simmons resented his intrusion into her life. However, Mrs. Simmons later hit bottom. She sought help through Alcoholics Anonymous and experienced a sudden Christian conversion. Having found sobriety, she returned to her pastor to talk with him about her experience. He completely rejected her experience. He told her that Alcoholics Anonymous was a substitute for faith in God and the church. He discounted also any sudden religious experience as merely evidence of emotional insecurity. Mrs. Simmons was crushed. Her pastor had assumed an authoritarian attitude toward her. When she refused his help and found help through Alcoholics Anonymous and the grace of God, he rejected her and castigated her experience. He demonstrated no understanding or patience toward his parishioner. She moved her membership to another church where she found understanding and acceptance. Other alcoholics and spouses of alcoholics commented upon this disturbingly uncommon kind of pastoral rejection.

The case of Mr. Kemp illustrates a different pastoral role. Mr. Kemp was active in his church. He thought that he was hiding his alcoholism from his pastor. Neither he nor the pastor ever mentioned it to each other. However, after his final surrender, he discovered that for the previous few months, his wife had been " camping out on the pastor's doorstep." She had been supported and comforted by the pastor's concern and understanding. Mr. Kemp was deeply appreciative of the pastor's " behind the scenes " help. The pastor was the first person he talked with after his surrender. He encouraged Mr. Kemp to become identified with Alcoholics Anonymous. He offered him his friendship and counsel in any way he could be of help. This pastor demonstrated the wisdom of letting the alcoholic take the initiative toward him. In the meantime, he was actively engaged in a ministry of supportive counseling with the wife. He was aware of his own limitations, the total needs of the alcoholic, and the availability of community resources. Pastoral pride did not interfere with his willingness to give support and guidance.

The case of Mrs. Pope shows another understanding, but more directive, role of a pastor. Mrs. Pope's pastor knew of her alcoholism and had talked with her about it. He was patient, and his visits did not threaten her. Two weeks after Mrs. Pope had experienced surrender, the pastor encouraged her to attend a meeting of Alcoholics Anonymous. She said she would not go by herself. Therefore, the pastor asked her if she would go with him to a meeting. She trusted the pastor and agreed to go with him. The next night he picked her up and went with her to her first meeting of Alcoholics Anonymous. She found genuine acceptance in this group and has become a very active member. She continues to have a durable relationship with her pastor. She attends church regularly. This pastor had formed the kind of faithful, trusting relationship with the parishioner which allowed him to take initiative toward her in her alcoholism. He introduced her to Alcoholics Anonymous while maintaining his own relationship with her. This is a vitally important role that the pastor can play.

The case of Mrs. Simmons is an example of pastoral ineffectiveness. Pastoral care was absent. The cases of Mr. Kemp and Mrs. Pope exemplify effective pastoral care through different procedures. These cases indicate that no legalistic rules can be set concerning what a pastor should do in every case. Each person's case is different. But the guidelines of understanding and sensitivity toward the alcoholic and his family, recognition of both strengths and limitations, and the awareness of community resources can apply to the pastoral role in every case of alcoholism in the parish.

The Authority of the Minister. The problem of whether or not a pastor should take initiative toward a practicing alcoholic brings up the question of the authority of the minister. The alcoholics in the sampling expressed a high regard for ministers who tried to understand and help the individual. They indicated that the minister's authority in dealing with the alcoholic rested upon his willingness to understand, without condemning, and his genuine concern for the individual. They suggested that the judgmental, authoritarian, unaccepting minister had forfeited his real authority to approach the alcoholic.

Daniel Day Williams sees the minister's authority rooted in the revelation in Jesus Christ. " This is to say that our authority derives from him whose claim rests finally on nothing other than the sheer expression of love to God and to men." [15] The alcoholic is sensitive to the genuine, unoffensive expression of concern. The minister whose authority is grounded in the love of God revealed in Jesus Christ does not seek to impose his will on the alcoholic. Rather, he seeks to free the imprisoned will of the alcoholic and walk with him toward a genuine Christian conversion. He forms a faithful, durable relationship which makes him a trust-

worthy friend in whom the alcoholic can confide. One recovered alcoholic, who had experienced difficulty with his
pastor, said that a minister must be willing to give nothing
but friendship to an alcoholic for as much as several years
before he can begin to give direct counsel. This insight suggests that pastoral patience is a prerequisite for pastoral
authority.

Pastoral authority involves pastoral judgment. Seward
Hiltner differentiates between judgment as " alienation "
and judgment as " shared appraisal." [16] Judgment alienates
the pastor from the alcoholic when it is imposed from without, as law. Pastoral authority may be used as a weapon
designed for punishment. It may be used as a defense with
which the pastor protects himself from real involvement in
the life of the alcoholic. Whether it is used as an offensive
or defensive weapon, pastoral judgment, in this sense, creates a deeper sense of isolation for the alcoholic.

This does not mean that there is no place for judgment.
Judgment as shared appraisal is not given as law, but as understanding. The alcoholic is his own judge. He has already
condemned himself. There is a great difference in the pastoral judgment that says, " You are guilty of ruining your
life and the life of your family," and that which says, " From
what you say, you seem to feel very guilty for the way you
have behaved in recent months." The latter judgment is an
appraisal shared with the alcoholic. It is expressing his own
feelings for him. It speaks from within, not from without.
It comes as understanding, not as law. It unites the thoughts
of the pastor with those of the alcoholic rather than creating
alienation. Wayne E. Oates sees this as the work of the
Holy Spirit, convincing the individual of judgment from
within the internal frame of reference. He concludes that
" the gift of sober judgment cannot be pasted on, nailed on,
or beaten into a person." [17]

E. Kinder writes that ministerial authority is tested by
the way in which the authority is exercised. The application
of authority must conform to the gospel of Christ as set forth

in the New Testament. The authority of Christ was rooted in his servanthood, not in his office. Kinder states that the only means the church has for asserting authority is through a " personal appeal to heart and conscience." [18] The church should exercise this authority with the hope that

> the " substance " of her real authority will be proved in " demonstration of the Spirit and of power " (I Cor. 2:4), by saving men from perversity and existential guilt and by reconciling them to God so that they may receive salvation.[19]

The Ministry of Introduction. Oates has described one of the major pastoral opportunities as " the ministry of introduction." [20] There are three aspects of this ministry. First, as a representative of God, the pastor introduces individuals to God as He is revealed in Jesus Christ. Secondly, the pastor is continually meeting persons and forming durable relationships with them. Thirdly, the pastor introduces individuals to each other and to persons " who can enable them to help themselves by providing them with the rich resources that friendship, professional skills, and clinical experience can afford them." [21]

The work of the pastor in the case of Mrs. Pope is the best example of the ministry of introduction. The pastor was sensitive to her fear of going alone to a meeting with a group of strangers. Knowing that she trusted him, the pastor took Mrs. Pope to the meeting and introduced her to the members of Alcoholics Anonymous. This group could offer her the kind of understanding she had not found elsewhere. As. Mrs. Pope's pastor demonstrates, the minister of introduction does not break his own relationship with the individual. Rather, he enriches the relationship through the inclusion of other concerned and helpful people. The clinical research shows that the ministry of introduction is one of the most valuable services a pastor can render his alcoholic parishioner.

V. New Signs of a Practical Ministry

As the case studies have pointed out, the alcoholic needs help. He cannot recover by himself. Neither can one organization, of any sort, meet all his needs. The parish fellowship is a group that can join a cooperative effort with other community resources in offering a practical ministry to the alcoholic. In the past, the church's activity in this field has been largely restricted to an advocation of temperance or prohibition. Not one recovered alcoholic in the sampling, however, considered the church's support of legal prohibition or the temperance movement as practical, workable means of combating alcoholism. It had no effect upon their consumption of alcohol or upon their sobriety. It sets the church up as a moral judge and further alienates those who are already isolated from its fellowship. Will Durant shares a personal confession which is relevant to the church at this point, in terms of the crusading zeal of many groups attempting to deal with the alcohol problem by abolishing alcohol. He says:

> I went forth to reform the world. I denounced the ways of mankind, and bemoaned the backwardness of my time. . . . But the world would not listen, and I grew bitter. I gathered anecdotes of human stupidity, and heralded the absurdities and injustices of men. One day, an enemy said, " You have in yourself all the faults which you scorn in others; you, too, are capable of selfishness and greed; and the world is what it is because men are what you are." I considered it in solitude, and found that it was true. Then it came to me that reform should begin at home; and since that day I have not had time to remake the world.[22]

It may well be that self-reformation within the church community is the most effective means of the reformation of those outside that community.

Moralistic legalism operates on the basis of the unreality

of illusion and the distortion of superstition. The illusion is that we can get rid of the human problems leading to alcoholism simply by getting rid of alcohol. This strategy has little effect upon the complex problem of alcoholism. It is unrealistic to suppose that modern society is going to give up alcohol. Alcohol has been here for generations, and it will continue to be here for generations to come. The church must recognize that fact. The superstition is that the substance of alcohol is " evil " in itself. Jesus had to combat this false concept of food and drink in those to whom he was speaking. Matthew, ch. 15, and Mark, ch. 7, record His admonition that sinfulness is that which comes out of the heart of man, not that which enters into his mouth. In spite of the clarity of the New Testament at this point, this ancient concept is behind much of the Protestant viewpoint concerning alcohol. Wayne Oates says:

> The hopeless struggle between the total abstainer's " devil-in-a-bottle " attitude toward the alcoholic and the alcoholic's feverish search for " God-in-a-bottle " is a deadlock. When the pious church member and the stubborn alcoholic call for the capitulation of each other, the total situation deteriorates.[23]

Even though it is obvious that alcohol consumption can compound personal problems and make life a disaster, it is equally obvious that the initial problems are within man and not within the substance of alcohol. They are problems that can be healed only through active concern and acceptance, not through alienating judgment and pious legalism. The church's ministry in the problem of alcoholism needs to be focused squarely upon the aspect of human redemption rather than on negative restrictions. The Christian community is called to give itself for the life of the world, not to demand that the world perfectly meet all its social and moral expectations. The gospel of Christ is the good news of gracious forgiveness and acceptance, not a law of legalistic demands. This study indicated two practical ways of

fighting alcoholism: educating the public on alcoholism
through churches, schools, civic groups, etc., and openly
attempting to rehabilitate the alcoholic.

The most hopeful sign, observed in the process of research, of the role of the church in ministering to the alcoholic was the creative work of a Methodist church. The
Commision of Christian Social Concerns of the Fourth Ave-
nue Methodist Church, Louisville, Kentucky, sponsors a
nonsectarian residence home for alcoholic men who have a
strong desire for continued sobriety. The home can accom-
modate approximately ten men. It is supervised by a resident
manager, who is also a recovered alcoholic. The men live in
an atmosphere of mutual trust and responsibility. They
share the cost of food and upkeep. Each man works at a
job in town. The church makes no demands upon the men.
The object is to give these men a place to live during their
readjustment in society, not to get their names on the church
rolls. Men are considered for the residence home upon the
recommendation of an understanding and reputable individual, a clergyman, or a social agency. No therapeutic program is offered. The alcoholics learn to live together in a
natural social environment.[24]

This creative ministry offers both of the most effective
methods of fighting alcoholism. In the first place, it helps
the alcoholic make his way back into society. He begins to
contribute to the welfare of others and learn personal responsibility. It gives him a community with which to identify. In the second place, this resident home is a means for
educating the parish fellowship on alcoholism. The members are exposed to the process, nature, and consequences
of alcoholism. They share in the struggle an alcoholic experiences in attempting to regain sobriety. It is a living
laboratory of human experience. This is always the best
teacher. The chairman of the Commission that sponsors the
home reported that the membership of the church has responded with enthusiasm to this ministry. They have said
that it has increased their understanding of alcoholism.

The Roman Catholic Church has provided a similar home for alcoholic priests. It is located in Lake Orion, Michigan, and accommodates eighteen priests. In this home, a therapeutic program is offered. The resident manager claims 80 percent success and the house physician claims 50 percent. Other such Catholic homes are being planned for the approximately four thousand alcoholic priests in the United States.[25]

During the process of this study, the author participated in a religious discussion group for alcoholics. The alcoholics in this group expressed a need to discuss religious problems in an open atmosphere. Alcoholics Anonymous does not meet this specific need. The group proved very helpful to those who had genuine religious questions. Enno K. Lohrmann reports the success he has witnessed after three and one-half years of leading such a group. The group agenda is varied and relatively unstructured. Group participation is encouraged.[26]

A religious discussion group is a ministry the parish fellowship can provide for alcoholics. It gives a small, intimate group within the church with which they can identify. It provides an open, free atmosphere for genuine dialogue. Hopefully, such a group would enable the alcoholics to grow in the Christian faith and strengthen them in their life of sobriety. A number of churches are undertaking this kind of practical ministry. The most important thing is a growing awareness that millions of people are suffering the degenerative effects of alcoholism while the churches stand by with little more than a few moral pronouncements to offer. This awareness must lead the Christian community into an active involvement with the sufferers of alcoholism, fulfilling the dynamic, redemptive meaning of the incarnation of Jesus Christ in the ministry of the church.

CHAPTER VI

Conclusions and Needs
for Further Research

HAVING DEVELOPED and discussed significant aspects of Christian experience in alcoholism, with the support of clinical evidence, we will enumerate in this chapter the conclusions that have been made in the study, and suggest areas that deserve additional research.

I. CONCLUSIONS

From the standpoint of research methodology, it was shown that clinical study of Christian experience in alcoholism, using the focused interview and case history methods of research, provides essential and reliable information on the problem of the conversion of the alcoholic in the context of the parish fellowship. Most recovered alcoholics are unusually willing to talk about their experience to someone who is concerned about them and their problem. The reliability of the responses can be checked through another person who knows the alcoholic well enough to validate the case history.

The research procedure supported the view that pastoral research is a function of pastoral care. As a recognized minister, the researcher should not attempt to escape his pastoral role. Effective pastoral research not only collects data, it also performs a ministry of concerned listening to and participating in the life of the individual. The pastoral researcher should endeavor to form a faithful friendship with the respondent, taking seriously his developmental pilgrimage, and giving him encouragement in his present circumstances. Elements of durability appeared in these research interviews, reflecting that under proper conditions alcoholics *can* begin to form durable relationships.

It was concluded that the experiences of conversion in alcoholism, explored in the sampling, fall into four categories: psychosocial conversion, restrictive Christian conversion, limited Christian conversion, and comprehensive Christian conversion. Psychosocial conversion is characterized by a release from alcohol addiction and improved interpersonal relationships. It has no visible religious interpretation. Restrictive Christian conversion is a redirecting of the compulsion to drink to the compulsion to become absorbed in a religious cause. The individual is legalistic, proud, and intolerant. In limited Christian conversion, the individual makes intellectual religious affirmations, but he makes no personal commitment. The surrender reaction is absent. Comprehensive Christian conversion is total, genuine conversion. It is characterized by surrender, a change of nature, and manifest fruits of conversion.

A fourth conclusion is that the dynamics of Christian conversion in alcoholism portray vividly a Christian understanding of the conversion experience. The dynamics of Christian conversion are often subtle and beneath the surface. They are remarkably observable, however, in the experience of the alcoholic. It becomes apparent that whether a conversion is gradual or sudden, it involves a consistent set of personality dynamics. The difference lies in the intensity, not in the quality, of the experience. The research showed pride to be a hindrance to conversion. Selfish, false pride must be changed into genuine humility for total conversion to occur. The process of this change is surrender. The way is open for the act of surrender when the individual feels a sense of shame or sin. Surrender is expressed through honest confession before God and man. The sense of forgiveness releases the person from guilt and enables him to move into a new life, free of self-destructive compulsions. Christian conversion is most meaningful to individuals who have lost hope. Hopelessness is replaced by hope. Early religious training enables an individual to experience genuine adult Christian conversion easier than is possible with no early religious training.

The Holy Spirit works within the internal frame of reference, using the dynamics of conversion to convict the person from within, and enabling him to surrender and to be redeemed. In Christian conversion the individual moves out of his diffused or negative identity into a clear, positive identity as a responsible person and a child of God. He finds a depth of meaning that fills the meaninglessness of his life. The validity of his conversion experience is evaluated by his ability to harmonize his true values with his behavior and interpersonal relations. Christian conversion gives direction, confidence, and inner strength to the individual who has suffered deprived parental relationships and family background. These dynamics present the conversion of the alcoholic as a model of Christian conversion.

A fifth conclusion is that the personality theories of András Angyal and Kazimierz Dabrowski provide a holistic frame of reference within which to build a model of the alcoholic experience. A study of these contemporary theories gives insight and understanding into the process of alcoholism. It reveals the conflictual nature of personality and the disturbances that occur when neurotic trends become dominant. It shows that although alcoholism is a self-destructive process, when it runs its full course and multilevel personality disintegration occurs, it may become the means of rebuilding the personality on a higher level of functioning. Conversion involves personality disequilibrium or disintegration. Old patterns must be surrendered before new, healthy ones can take shape in the personality. Thus, the personality disintegration involved in alcoholism may have a highly positive, rather than a negative, outcome.

Lastly, this study concludes that although the parish fellowship does have a role in the recovery from alcoholism, it is usually a relatively ineffective community in meeting the basic needs of the alcoholic. The alcoholic generally perceives the church as an institution of religious teaching and spiritual guidance. Only in a low percentage of cases is the church seen as an open, supportive fellowship. Personal feelings, religious orientations, and social-class factors condition the relationship between the parish and the alcoholic. The alcoholic's deep need for community is most effectively met by Alcoholics Anonymous. Nevertheless, Alcoholics Anonymous cannot meet all the needs of the alcoholic. If the parish fellowship can overcome its prejudices and confess its own problems, then it can offer understanding and acceptance to the alcoholic. The alcoholic needs the spiritual guidance offered by the church. When this is given with openness and concern, he may find support and strength in the parish relationships. The church can enhance its ministry to the alcoholic through cooperation with Alcoholics Anonymous.

The lack of pastoral care in the ministry to alcoholics is due, primarily, to the lack of understanding of alcoholism prevalent among ministers. The authority of the minister in dealing with the alcoholic is based on his willingness to understand and to serve, not upon his office. This is consistent with the authority of Christ. Although the minister may be limited in his relationship to the alcoholic, he can usually perform the ministry of introduction. He should introduce the alcoholic to those groups and persons who can mean the most to him. The supreme function of this ministry is the introduction of the alcoholic to the healing, redeeming love of Jesus Christ.

The church's ministry to the alcoholic is not enhanced by ethical moralisms and judgmental pronouncements. It must engage in a practical, " hand-to-hand combat " ministry. Lay alcohol education and alcoholic rehabilitation are most consistent with the true Christian concepts of understanding and love. A ministry that combines both of these aspects is the most effective method of fulfilling the role of the Christian community in the recovery from alcoholism.

II. Needs for Further Research

Problems arose during the research that are outside the scope of this study. Additional investigation of these problems would add insight and understanding to Christian experience in alcoholism.

The research procedure followed in this study pointed out the importance of the relationship between the pastoral researcher and the respondent. This needs further investigation. There frequently seems to be a dichotomy between the identities of pastor and research scholar. Is this a valid assumption? This writer thinks not. A conclusion of this study is that pastoral research is a function of pastoral care. *Objectivity does not mean insensitivity.* A research project that explored carefully the role of the pastor as a clinical researcher and pinpointed the interpersonal dynamics involved would be a valuable asset to research methodology in pastoral care.

The categories of conversion that are defined in this book need further testing. It would be helpful if these categories could be tested by application to conversion experiences in circumstances other than alcoholism. It may be that other categories could be found which were not apparent in this research.

Although Howard J. Clinebell, Jr., has published some research in the area of the attitudes of the clergy toward alcoholism, this needs deeper study. This project revealed that a number of alcoholics are not helped by the church because of the authoritarian, insensitive attitudes of ministers. Clinebell's questionnaire survey needs to be explored further by means of interviews with a sampling of Protestant clergymen. The interviews could take place with ministers who are antagonistic toward the alcoholic, and with those who are understanding and helpful. Such a study would give deeper insight into the relationship between the church and the alcoholic.

Another area where further research is needed is the role of the church in alcoholic rehabilitation. Such services as the residence home for alcoholics, discussed in Chapter V, are new and scarce. They are still experimental in nature. As these services grow and develop in churches, they need to be studied and evaluated. An excellent project would be the working out of a total program of ministry to alcoholics. A similar study needs to be made of the role of the denomination in alcoholic rehabilitation.

There are also those alcoholics who experience religious conversion completely outside the framework of organized religion. A study of men converted in rescue missions and other such locations would add new information on the phenomenon of religious conversion. It became apparent during this study that some rescue missions are very hostile toward the clergy and organized religion. They express pride in " delivering men from the sins of drink and tobacco." These experiences were observed, but they are outside the context of this project. A study in that kind of setting is another project.

These suggestions indicate the varieties of problems encountered in a study of religious experience in alcoholism. One study cannot begin to explore them all. Each project is limited, but each contributes valuable knowledge to a complicated but rewarding field of research. The hope of this researcher is that the present study will inspire others to explore even more deeply this laboratory of human experience.

Notes

CHAPTER I

Introduction

1. For an interesting discussion of the dramatic quality of alcoholism, see: Eric Berne, *Games People Play: The Psychology of Human Relationships* (Grove Press, Inc., 1964), pp. 73–81.

2. Seldon D. Bacon, "The Rutgers Center of Alcohol Studies: A Tentative Conceptualization of Purpose," *Quarterly Journal of Studies on Alcohol*, Vol. XXIII (1962), p. 322.

3. Francis W. McPeek, "The Role of Religious Bodies in the Treatment of Inebriety in the United States," *Alcohol, Science and Society: Twenty-nine Lectures with Discussions as Given at the Yale Summer School of Alcohol Studies* (Quarterly Journal of Studies on Alcohol, 1945), p. 417.

4. Howard J. Clinebell, Jr., *Understanding and Counseling the Alcoholic: Through Religion and Psychology* (Abingdon Press, 1956), p. 149.

5. Frank Stagg, *New Testament Theology* (Broadman Press, 1962), pp. 145–146.

6. William James, *The Varieties of Religious Experience: A Study in Human Nature* (Collier Books, Crowell-Collier Publishing Co., 1961), p. 165.

7. Charles R. Stinnette, Jr., *Anxiety and Faith: Toward Resolving Anxiety in Christian Community* (The Seabury Press, Inc., 1955), p. 111.

8. Edgar Y. Mullins, *Talks on Soul Winning* (The Sunday School Board of the Southern Baptist Convention, 1920), p. 34.

9. Edgar Y. Mullins, *The Christian Religion in Its Doctrinal Expression* (Judson Press, 1917), p. 377.

10. *Ibid.*

11. Mark Keller and John R. Seeley, *The Alcohol Language: With a Selected Vocabulary* (Toronto: University of Toronto Press, 1958), p. 19.

12. Alfred Agrin, "Alcoholism — A Psychiatric Point of View," *Georgia Looks at Alcoholism* (6th ed.; Georgia Department of Public Health, Division of Mental Health, Alcoholic Rehabilitation Service, 1963), p. 18.

13. Daniel Day Williams, *The Minister and the Care of Souls* (Harper & Brothers, 1961), p. 123.

14. Samuel Southard, *Conversion and Christian Character* (Broadman Press, 1965), p. 44.

CHAPTER II

Categories of Conversion in Alcoholism

1. James, *op. cit.*, p. 160.

2. *Ibid.*, p. 165.

3. Earl H. Furgeson, "The Definition of Religious Conversion," *Pastoral Psychology*, Vol. XVI (September, 1965), pp. 8–16.

4. *Ibid.*, p. 15.

5. Walter Houston Clark, "William James: Contributions to the Psychology of Religious Conversion," *Pastoral Psychology*, Vol. XVI (September, 1965), pp. 29–36.

6. *Ibid.*, p. 30.

7. *Ibid.*

8. Harry M. Tiebout, "Conversion as a Psychological Phenomena in the Treatment of the Alcoholic," *Pastoral Psychology*, Vol. II (April, 1951), p. 28.

9. Harry M. Tiebout, "Alcoholics Anonymous — An Experiment of Nature," *Quarterly Journal of Studies on Alcohol*, Vol. XXII (1961), p. 53.

10. *Ibid.*

11. *Ibid.*
12. James, *op. cit.*, p. 202.
13. *Ibid.*
14. *Ibid.*
15. *Ibid.*
16. The cases of Mr. Mallory and Mr. Goode were obtained outside of the formal research procedure in this study, and should not be confused with the cases of Christian conversion.
17. William Sargant, *Battle for the Mind* (Doubleday & Company, Inc., 1957).
18. Wayne E. Oates, *Religious Factors in Mental Illness* (Association Press, 1955), p. 46.
19. *Ibid.*
20. Leon Salzman, " The Psychology of Regressive Religious Conversion," *The Journal of Pastoral Care*, Vol. VIII (1954), pp. 61–75.
21. David E. Roberts, *Psychotherapy and a Christian View of Man* (Charles Scribner's Sons, 1950), pp. 124–128.
22. *Ibid.*
23. Jonathan Edwards, *Religious Affections*, ed. by John E. Smith (Yale University Press, 1959), pp. 340–344.
24. *Ibid.*, p. 341.
25. *Ibid.*, p. 342.
26. András Angyal, *Foundations for a Science of Personality* (Commonwealth Fund, Division of Publications, 1941), p. 329.
27. Reinhold Niebuhr, *The Nature and Destiny of Man* (2 vols. in 1; Charles Scribner's Sons, 1949), Vol. I, p. 188.
28. Wayne E. Oates, *Protestant Pastoral Counseling* (The Westminster Press, 1962), p. 197.
29. *Ibid.*
30. Salzman, " The Psychology of Regressive Religious Conversion," *loc. cit.*, p. 73.
31. Eric Hoffer, *The True Believer: Thoughts on the Nature of Mass Movements* (The New American Library of World Literature, Inc., 1958), p. 51.
32. Furgeson, " The Definition of Religious Conversion," *loc. cit.*
33. Anton T. Boisen, *The Exploration of the Inner World: A Study of Mental Disorder and Religious Experience* (Wil-

let, Clark & Company, 1936), p. 51.

34. Oates, *Protestant Pastoral Counseling*, p. 201.

35. *Ibid.*, p. 202.

36. *Ibid.*, p. 203.

37. Oates, *Religious Factors in Mental Illness*, pp. 127–129.

38. Anton T. Boisen, *Problems in Religion and Life* (Abingdon-Cokesbury Press, 1946), p. 112.

39. James, *op. cit.*, p. 196.

40. Clark, "William James: Contributions to the Psychology of Religious Conversion," *loc. cit.*, p. 32.

41. James, *op. cit.*, p. 160.

42. Williams, *op. cit.*, p. 41.

43. Henry Nelson Wieman and Regina Westcott-Wieman, *Normative Psychology of Religion* (Thomas Y. Crowell Company, 1935), p. 163.

44. Roberts, *op. cit.*, pp. 129–143.

45. *Ibid.*, p. 132.

46. Herbert A. Tyson, "Elements of Religious Experience," *Journal of Religion and Health*, Vol. IV (1965), pp. 441–447.

47. Prescott Lecky, "The Personality," *The Self: Explorations in Personal Growth*, ed. by Clark E. Moustakas (Harper & Brothers, 1956), p. 89.

48. *Ibid.*, p. 91.

49. *Ibid.*

50. Anton T. Boisen, *Religion in Crisis and Custom* (Harper & Brothers, 1955), p. 186.

51. Angyal, *Foundations for a Science of Personality*, pp. 20–55 and 167–207. This is discussed at length in Chapter III.

52. Gordon W. Allport, *The Individual and His Religion* (The Macmillan Company, 1960).

53. Samuel Southard, *Pastoral Evangelism* (Broadman Press, 1962), pp. 20–21.

54. *Ibid.*, p. 21.

55. Williams, *op. cit.*, pp. 26–29.

56. *Ibid.*, p. 27.

57. *Ibid.*

58. Charles R. Stinnette, Jr., *Grace and the Searching of*

Our Hearts (Association Press, 1962), pp. 11–13.
   59. *Ibid.*, p. 12.
   60. *Ibid.*
   61. Furgeson, "The Definition of Religious Conversion,"
loc. cit.

CHAPTER III

Dynamics of Christian Experience in Alcoholism

   1. Mullins, *Talks on Soul Winning*, p. 18.
   2. Southard, *Conversion and Christian Character*, pp. 12 f.
   3. Mullins, *Talks on Soul Winning*, p. 19.
   4. James Bissett Pratt, *The Religious Consciousness: A Psychological Study* (The Macmillan Company, 1920), p. 123.
   5. Niebuhr, *op. cit.*
   6. Karen Horney, *Neurosis and Human Growth: The Struggle Toward Self-realization*, Vol. II: *The Collected Works of Karen Horney* (2 vols.; W. W. Norton & Company, Inc., 1963), p. 86.
   7. *Ibid.*, p. 90.
   8. *Ibid.*, p. 91.
   9. *Ibid.*, p. 106.
   10. Niebuhr, *op cit.*, p. 234.
   11. Horney, *op. cit.*, pp. 110–112.
   12. Erich Fromm, *The Heart of Man: Its Genius for Good and Evil* (Harper & Row, Publishers, Inc., 1964), p. 81.
   13. Harry M. Tiebout, "The Act of Surrender in the Therapeutic Process with Special Reference to Alcoholism," *Quarterly Journal of Studies on Alcohol*, Vol. X (1949), p. 50.
   14. *Ibid.*, p. 54.
   15. *Ibid.*, p. 56.
   16. Angyal, *Foundations for a Science of Personality*.
   17. András Angyal, *Neurosis and Treatment: A Holistic Theory*, ed. by E. Hanfmann and R. M. Jones (John Wiley & Sons, Inc., 1965), p. 107. Quotations are used by permission of the publisher.
   18. Martin D. Kissen, "Treatment of Alcoholics," *Quarterly Journal of Studies on Alcohol*, Supplement No. I (November, 1961), p. 104.

19. Mullins, *The Christian Religion in Its Doctrinal Expression,* p. 64.

20. Russell L. Dicks, "The Alcoholic and a Sense of Dignity," *Social Action,* Vol. XXIII (May, 1957), p. 9.

21. Abraham H. Maslow, "Personality Problems and Personality Growth," in Moustakas, ed., *op. cit.,* p. 236.

22. Helen Merrell Lynd, *On Shame and the Search for Identity* (Science Editions, 1962), p. 34.

23. Kazimierz Dabrowski, *Positive Disintegration,* ed. by Jason Aronson (Little, Brown and Company, 1964), p. 35.

24. John Dollard, "Drinking Mores of Social Classes," *Alcohol, Science and Society: Twenty-nine Lectures,* p. 99.

25. Mullins, *The Christian Religion in Its Doctrinal Expression,* p. 289.

26. Marc Oraison, "Psychology and the Sense of Sin," *Sin,* Marc Oraison *et al.,* tr. by Bernard Murchland, C.S.C., and Raymond Meyerpeter, O.S.B. (The Macmillan Company, 1962), p. 29.

27. *Ibid.*

28. *Ibid.*

29. Seward Hiltner, *Preface to Pastoral Theology* (Abingdon Press, 1958), p. 41.

30. Clinebell, *op. cit.,* pp. 128–129. This book contains an excellent discussion of the program of Alcoholics Anonymous.

31. Max Thurian, *Confession,* tr. by Edwin Hudson (London: SCM Press, Ltd., 1958), p. 68.

32. *Ibid.*

33. *Ibid.*

34. Paul W. Pruyser, "Phenomenology and Dynamics of Hoping," *Journal for the Scientific Study of Religion,* Vol. III (1963), p. 94.

35. Gabriel Marcel, *Homo Viator: Introduction to a Metaphysic of Hope,* tr. by Emma Craufurd (Harper Torchbooks, Harper & Row, Publishers, Inc., 1962), p. 36.

36. *Ibid.,* p. 31.

37. *Ibid.,* p. 47.

38. Erik H. Erikson, *Insight and Responsibility: Lectures on the Ethical Implications of Psychoanalytic Insight* (W. W. Norton & Company, Inc., 1964), p. 115.

39. *Ibid.*

40. *Ibid.*, p. 116.

41. Emil Brunner, *Eternal Hope,* tr. by Harold Knight (The Westminster Press, 1954), p. 7.

42. John H. Flavell, *The Developmental Psychology of Jean Piaget* (D. Van Nostrand Company, Inc., 1963), p. 271.

43. Wayne E. Oates, *Christ and Selfhood* (Association Press, 1961), p. 139.

44. Edwards, *op. cit.,* p. 205.

45. Oates, *Christ and Selfhood,* p. 145.

46. Wayne E. Oates, " The Holy Spirit and the Overseer of the Flock," *Review and Expositor,* Vol. LXIII (Spring, 1966), p. 189.

47. *Ibid.*, p. 195.

48. Maslow in Moustakas, ed., *op. cit.,* p. 234.

49. Erik H. Erikson, *Identity and the Life Cycle* (Psychological Issues, Monograph, Vol. I, No. 1. International Universities Press, Inc., 1959), p. 89.

50. *Ibid.*

51. *Ibid.*, p. 113.

52. Søren Kierkegaard, *Fear and Trembling; and, Sickness Unto Death,* tr. by Walter Lowrie (Doubleday & Company, Inc., 1954), pp. 168–175.

53. Robert J. Gibbins and Richard H. Walters, " Three Preliminary Studies of a Psychoanalytic Theory of Alcohol Addiction," *Quarterly Journal of Studies on Alcohol,* Vol. XXI (1960), pp. 618–641.

54. Erikson, *Identity and the Life Cycle,* pp. 129–132.

55. *Ibid.*, p. 132.

56. Karl A. Menninger, *Man Against Himself* (Harcourt, Brace & Company, Inc., 1938), p. 181.

57. *Ibid.*, p. 184.

58. Gardner Murphy, *Personality: A Biosocial Approach to Origins and Structure* (Harper & Brothers, 1947), p. 520.

59. Donald S. Berry, " Alcohol and Traffic," *Alcohol, Science and Society: Twenty-nine Lectures,* p. 156. This figure was also given as a current percentage by Dr. Norman A. Desrosiers, then Director of Medical Services, West Virginia Department of Mental Health, Charleston, West Virginia. The author heard Dr. Desrosiers speak at a closed meeting of community leaders on January 19, 1966, in Louisville, Kentucky.

60. Zanie Ruth Adams, " The Alcoholic's Empty Cup," *Inventory: A Bi-Monthly Journal on Alcohol and Alcoholism,* Vol. XV (July–August, 1965), p. 2.

61. Viktor E. Frankl, *Man's Search for Meaning: An Introduction to Logotherapy,* tr. by Ilse Lasch (rev. ed.; Beacon Press, 1963), p. 108.

62. Viktor E. Frankl, *The Doctor and the Soul: An Introduction to Logotherapy,* tr. by Richard and Clara Winston (Alfred A. Knopf, Inc., 1955), p. 147.

63. Boisen, *Religion in Crisis and Custom,* pp. 47–48.

64. Cf. E. M. Jellinek, " Heredity of the Alcoholic," *Alcohol, Science and Society: Twenty-nine Lectures,* pp. 105–114.

CHAPTER IV

Christian Conversion and Personality Theory

1. Before his premature death, Dr. Angyal had received his Ph.D. in Psychology from the University of Vienna and his M.D. from the University of Turin. He served on the staff at Worcester State Hospital as research psychiatrist. While in private practice, he was affiliated with the Yale Center of Alcohol Studies. His last position, assumed in 1953, was Psychiatric Consultant of the Psychological Counseling Center of Brandeis University.

2. Angyal, *Neurosis and Treatment,* p. xvi. This posthumously published book contains a comprehensive summary of Angyal's contributions. It is the basic resource for this chapter.

3. *Ibid.,* p. 5.

4. *Ibid.*

5. Angyal, *Foundations for a Science of Personality,* p. 41. This book is Angyal's earlier theoretical writing. It is a secondary resource for this chapter.

6. Angyal, *Neurosis and Treatment,* p. 17.

7. *Ibid.*

8. *Ibid.,* p. 10.

9. *Ibid.,* p. 15.

10. *Ibid.*

11. *Ibid.*

12. *Ibid.,* p. 21.

13. Angyal, *Foundations for a Science of Personality,* p. 101.
14. *Ibid.*
15. Angyal, *Neurosis and Treatment,* p. 58.
16. " Gestalt " is a psychological term meaning " configuration," " shape," or " organization." It is made up of interrelated parts, but the whole exceeds a mere summation of its parts.
17. Angyal, *Neurosis and Treatment,* p. 63.
18. *Ibid.,* p. 63.
19. *Ibid.,* p. 64.
20. *Ibid.*
21. *Ibid.,* p. 65.
22. *Ibid.*
23. *Ibid.,* p. 67.
24. *Ibid.*
25. Angyal, *Foundations for a Science of Personality,* p. 7.
26. Angyal, *Neurosis and Treatment,* p. 71.
27. *Ibid.*
28. *Ibid.,* p. 72.
29. *Ibid.*
30. *Ibid.*
31. *Ibid.,* p. 73.
32. *Ibid.,* p. 81.
33. *Ibid.,* p. 82.
34. *Ibid.,* p. 83.
35. *Ibid.*
36. *Ibid.,* p. 99.
37. *Ibid.,* p. 103.
38. *Ibid.,* p. 104.
39. *Ibid.,* p. 105.
40. *Ibid.,* p. 157.
41. *Ibid.*
42. *Ibid.*
43. *Ibid.*
44. *Ibid.,* p. 177.
45. *Ibid.,* p. 178.
46. Erikson, *Identity and the Life Cycle,* pp. 129–132.
47. Angyal, *Neurosis and Treatment,* p. 173.
48. Desrosiers, *loc. cit.,* Ch. IV, n. 59.
49. Angyal, *Neurosis and Treatment,* p. 179.

50. *Ibid.*, p. 181.
51. *Ibid.*, p. 221.
52. *Ibid.*
53. *Ibid.*
54. *Ibid.*, p. 254.
55. *Ibid.*, p. 255.
56. *Ibid.*
57. Kazimierz Dabrowski is a professor in the Polish Academy of Science and the Director of the Institute of Children's Psychiatry and Mental Hygiene, Warsaw, Poland. He received his M.D. at the University of Geneva Medical School in 1929 and a Ph.D. in experimental psychology from the University of Poznán in 1932. He studied under such men as Jean Piaget and Wilhelm Stekel. Although he has written extensively, his first book to be translated into English is *Positive Disintegration*.
58. Dabrowski, *op. cit.*, p. xiv.
59. *Ibid.*, p. 3.
60. Boisen, *Problems in Religion and Life*, p. 112.
61. Dabrowski, *op. cit.*, pp. 5–6.
62. *Ibid.*, p. 6.
63. *Ibid.*, p. 7.
64. *Ibid.*, p. 8.
65. *Ibid.*, p. 10.
66. *Ibid.*
67. *Ibid.*, p. 19.
68. *Ibid.*, p. 21.
69. *Ibid.*
70. *Ibid.*, p. 21.
71. *Ibid.*, p. 33.
72. *Ibid.*, p. 35.
73. *Ibid.*, p. 36.
74. *Ibid.*, p. 39.
75. Alfred Adler, *The Individual Psychology of Alfred Adler: A Systematic Presentation in Selections from His Writings*, ed. by Heinz L. Ansbacher and Rowena R. Ansbacher (Basic Books, Inc., Publishers, 1956).
76. Dabrowski, *op. cit.*, p. 45.
77. *Ibid.*, p. 53.
78. *Ibid.*, p. 59.
79. *Ibid.*

80. *Ibid.,* p. 61.
81. *Ibid.,* p. 62.

CHAPTER V

Christian Community and Recovery from Alcoholism

1. Arnold S. Linsky, " Religious Differences in Lay Attitudes and Knowledge on Alcoholism and Its Treatment,"
Journal for the Scientific Study of Religion, Vol. V (Fall,
1965), p. 41.
2. Dollard, " Drinking Mores of Social Classes," *loc. cit.,*
p. 100.
3. *Ibid.,* p. 99.
4. Linsky, " Religious Differences in Lay Attitudes and
Knowledge on Alcoholism and Its Treatment," *loc. cit.,* p. 48.
5. Dollard, " Drinking Mores of Social Classes," *loc. cit.*
6. Angyal, *Neurosis and Treatment,* p. 15.
7. Paul E. Johnson, *The Psychology of Religion* (rev. ed.;
Abingdon Press, 1959), p. 277.
8. Herbert A. Raskin, " Psychiatric Aspects of Alcoholism,"
Inventory: A Bi-Monthly Journal on Alcohol and Alcoholism,
Vol. XV (November–December, 1965), p. 10.
9. Johnson, *op. cit.,* p. 279.
10. Dietrich Bonhoeffer, *Life Together,* tr. by John W.
Doberstein (Harper & Brothers, 1954), p. 20.
11. Kahlil Gibran, in Aly Wassil, *The Wisdom of Christ*
(Harper & Row, Publishers, Inc., 1965), p. 107.
12. Clinebell, *op. cit.,* p. 110.
13. *Ibid.*
14. *Ibid.,* pp. 157–245. One third of Clinebell's book is a
discussion of the attitudes and the role of the minister in the
problem of alcoholism.
15. Williams, *op. cit.,* p. 50.
16. Seward Hiltner, " Judgment and Appraisal in Pastoral
Care," *Pastoral Psychology,* Vol. XVI (December, 1965), pp.
41–47.
17. Oates, " The Holy Spirit and the Overseer of the
Flock," *loc. cit.,* p. 195.
18. E. Kinder, " The Authority of Christ in His Church,"

Authority and the Church, ed. by R. R. Williams (London: S.P.C.K., 1965), p. 44.

19. *Ibid.*

20. Wayne E. Oates, *The Christian Pastor* (rev. ed.; The Westminster Press, 1964), pp. 220–236.

21. *Ibid.,* pp. 220–221.

22. Will Durant, in Wassil, *op. cit.*

23. Wayne E. Oates, *Alcohol: In and Out of the Church* (Broadman Press, 1966), p. 131.

24. The author learned of this residence home through talking with the chairman of the Commission in the church and with the resident manager. It has been in operation since January, 1965. According to the manager, it is the only such home in existence.

25. "Whisky Priests," *Newsweek,* Vol. LXVII (January 10, 1966), p. 58.

26. Enno K. Lohrmann, "A Religious Discussion Group for Alcoholics," *Inventory: A Bi-Monthly Journal on Alcohol and Alcoholism,* Vol. XV (September–October, 1965), pp. 5–7, 10–11.

Selected Bibliography

A. *Books*

Alcohol, Science and Society: Twenty-nine Lectures with Discussions as Given at the Yale Summer School of Alcohol Studies. Quarterly Journal of Studies on Alcohol, 1945.

Allport, Gordon W., *The Individual and His Religion: A Psychological Interpretation.* The Macmillan Company, 1960.

Angyal, András, *Foundations for a Science of Personality.* Commonwealth Fund, Division of Publications, 1941.

—— *Neurosis and Treatment: A Holistic Theory,* ed. by E. Hanfmann and R. M. Jones. John Wiley & Sons, Inc., 1965.

Boisen, Anton T., *The Exploration of the Inner World: A Study of Mental Disorder and Religious Experience.* Willet, Clark & Company, 1936; Harper Torchbooks, Harper & Row, Publishers, Inc., 1962.

—— *Problems in Religion and Life.* Abingdon-Cokesbury Press, 1946.

—— *Religion in Crisis and Custom.* Harper & Brothers, 1955.

Bonhoeffer, Dietrich, *Life Together,* tr. by John W. Doberstein. Harper & Brothers, 1954.

Brunner, Emil, *Eternal Hope,* tr. by Harold Knight. The Westminster Press, 1954.

Clinebell, Howard J., Jr., *Understanding and Counseling the Alcoholic: Through Religion and Psychology.* Abingdon Press, 1956.

Dabrowski, Kazimierz, *Positive Disintegration*, ed. by Jason Aronson. Little, Brown and Company, 1964.

Edwards, Jonathan, *Religious Affections*, ed. by John E. Smith. Yale University Press, 1959.

Erikson, Erik H., *Identity and the Life Cycle*. (Psychological Issues, Monograph, Vol. I, No. 1.) International Universities Press, Inc., 1959.

—— *Insight and Responsibility: Lectures on the Ethical Implications of Psychoanalytic Insight*. W. W. Norton & Company, Inc., 1964.

Ferm, Robert O., *The Psychology of Christian Conversion*. Fleming H. Revell Co., 1959.

Flavell, John H., *The Developmental Psychology of Jean Piaget*. D. Van Nostrand Company, Inc., 1963.

Frankl, Viktor E., *The Doctor and the Soul: An Introduction to Logotherapy*, tr. by Richard and Clara Winston. Alfred A. Knopf, Inc., 1955.

—— *Man's Search for Meaning: An Introduction to Logotherapy*, tr. by Ilse Lasch, rev. ed. Beacon Press, 1963.

Fromm, Erich, *The Heart of Man: Its Genius for Good and Evil*. Harper & Row, Publishers, Inc., 1964.

Georgia Looks at Alcoholism, 6th ed. Georgia Department of Public Health, Division of Mental Health, Alcoholic Rehabilitation Service, 1963.

Hiltner, Seward, *Preface to Pastoral Theology*. Abingdon Press, 1958.

Hoffer, Eric, *The True Believer: Thoughts on the Nature of Mass Movements*. The New American Library of World Literature, Inc., 1958.

Horney, Karen, *The Collected Works of Karen Horney*, Vol. II. W. W. Norton & Company, Inc., 1963.

James, William, *The Varieties of Religious Experience: A Study in Human Nature*. Collier Books, Crowell-Collier Publishing Co., 1961.

Johnson, Paul E., *The Psychology of Religion*, rev. ed. Abingdon Press, 1959.

Keller, Mark, and Seeley, John R., *The Alcohol Language: With a Selected Vocabulary*. Toronto: University of Toronto Press, 1958.

Kierkegaard, Søren, *Fear and Trembling; and, Sickness Unto*

Death, tr. by Walter Lowrie. Doubleday & Company, Inc., 1954.

Lecky, Prescott, *Self-consistency: A Theory of Personality,* ed. by Frederick C. Thorne. Island Press Co-operative, Inc., 1951.

Lynd, Helen Merrell, *On Shame and the Search for Identity.* Science Editions, 1962.

Marcel, Gabriel, *Homo Viator: Introduction to a Metaphysic of Hope,* tr. by Emma Craufurd. Harper & Row, Publishers, Inc., Harper Torchbooks, 1962.

Menninger, Karl A., *Man Against Himself.* Harcourt, Brace and Company, 1938.

Moustakas, Clark E., ed., *The Self: Explorations in Personal Growth.* Harper & Brothers, 1956.

Mullins, Edgar Y., *The Christian Religion in Its Doctrinal Expression.* Judson Press, 1917.

—— *Talks on Soul Winning.* The Sunday School Board of the Southern Baptist Convention, 1920.

Niebuhr, Reinhold, *The Nature and Destiny of Man,* 2 vols. in 1. Charles Scribner's Sons, 1949.

Oates, Wayne E., *Alcohol: In and Out of the Church.* Broadman Press, 1966.

—— *Christ and Selfhood.* Association Press, 1961.

—— *The Christian Pastor,* rev. ed. The Westminster Press, 1964.

—— *Protestant Pastoral Counseling.* The Westminster Press, 1962.

—— *Religious Factors in Mental Illness.* Association Press, 1955.

Oraison, Marc, *et al., Sin,* tr. by Bernard Murchland, C.S.C., and Raymond Meyerpeter, O.S.B. The Macmillan Company, 1962.

Roberts, David E., *Psychotherapy and a Christian View of Man.* Charles Scribner's Sons, 1950.

Sargant, William, *Battle for the Mind.* Doubleday & Company, Inc., 1957.

Sherrill, Lewis Joseph, *Guilt and Redemption,* rev. ed. John Knox Press, 1945.

Southard, Samuel, *Conversion and Christian Character.* Broadman Press, 1965.

—— *Pastoral Evangelism.* Broadman Press, 1962.

Stagg, Frank, *New Testament Theology.* Broadman Press, 1962.

Stinnette, Charles R., Jr., *Anxiety and Faith: Toward Resolving Anxiety in Christian Community.* The Seabury Press, Inc., 1955.

—— *Grace and the Searching of Our Heart.* Association Press, 1962.

Thouless, Robert H., *An Introduction to the Psychology of Religion.* London: Cambridge University Press, 1961.

Thurian, Max, *Confession,* tr. by Edwin Hudson. London: SCM Press, Ltd., 1958.

Warner, W. Lloyd, Meeker, Marchia, and Eells, Kenneth, *Social Class in America: A Manual of Procedure for the Measurement of Social Status.* Science Research Associates, 1949.

Wieman, Henry Nelson, and Westcott-Wieman, Regina, *Normative Psychology of Religion.* Thomas Y. Crowell Company, 1935.

Williams, Daniel Day, *The Minister and the Care of Souls.* Harper & Brothers, 1961.

Williams, R. R., ed., *Authority and the Church.* London: S.P.C.K., 1965.

B. *Articles*

Adams, Zanie Ruth, "The Alcoholic's Empty Cup," *Inventory: A Bi-Monthly Journal on Alcohol and Alcoholism,* Vol. XV (July–August, 1965), pp. 2–3, 12.

Bacon, Seldon D., "The Rutgers Center of Alcohol Studies: A Tentative Conceptualization of Purpose," *Quarterly Journal of Studies on Alcohol,* Vol. XXIII (1962), pp. 321–324.

Clark, Walter Houston, "William James: Contributions to the Psychology of Religious Conversion," *Pastoral Psychology,* Vol. XVI (September, 1965), pp. 29–36.

Dicks, Russell L., "The Alcoholic and a Sense of Dignity," *Social Action,* Vol. XXIII (May, 1957), pp. 6–11.

Furgeson, Earl H., "The Definition of Religious Conversion," *Pastoral Psychology,* Vol. XVI (September, 1965), pp. 8–16.

Gibbins, Robert J., and Walters, Richard H., "Three Preliminary Studies of a Psychoanalytic Theory of Alcohol Addic-

tion," *Quarterly Journal of Studies on Alcohol,* Vol. XXI
(1960), pp. 618–641.

Hiltner, Seward, "Judgment and Appraisal in Pastoral Care,"
Pastoral Psychology, Vol. XVI (December, 1965), pp. 41–
47.

Kildahl, John P., "The Personalities of Sudden Religious Converts," *Pastoral Psychology,* Vol. XVI (September, 1965),
pp. 37–44.

Kissen, Martin D., "Treatment of Alcoholics," *Quarterly Journal of Studies on Alcohol,* Supplement No. 1 (November,
1961), pp. 104–105.

Klink, Thomas W., "Some Categories of Religious Data Significant for the Clinician," *Journal of Pastoral Care,* Vol. XVI
(Summer, 1962), pp. 72–80.

Linsky, Arnold S., "Religious Differences in Lay Attitudes and
Knowledge on Alcoholism and Its Treatment," *Journal for
the Scientific Study of Religion,* Vol. V (Fall, 1965), pp.
41–50.

Lohrmann, Enno K., "A Religious Discussion Group for Alcoholics," *Inventory: A Bi-Monthly Journal on Alcohol and
Alcoholism,* Vol. XV (September–October, 1965), pp. 5–7,
10–11.

Oates, Wayne E., "The Holy Spirit and the Overseer of the
Flock," *Review and Expositor,* Vol. LXIII (Spring, 1966),
pp. 187–197.

Raskin, Herbert A., "Psychiatric Aspects of Alcoholism," *Inventory: A Bi-Monthly Journal on Alcohol and Alcoholism,*
Vol. XV (November–December, 1965), pp. 8–14, 31.

Salzman, Leon, "The Psychology of Regressive Religious Conversion," *The Journal of Pastoral Care,* Vol. VIII (1954),
pp. 61–75.

Tiebout, Harry M., "The Act of Surrender in the Therapeutic
Process with Special Reference to Alcoholism," *Quarterly
Journal of Studies on Alcohol,* Vol. X (1949), pp. 48–58.

—— "Alcoholics Anonymous — An Experiment of Nature,"
Quarterly Journal of Studies on Alcohol, Vol. XXII (1961),
pp. 52–68.

—— "Conversion as a Psychological Phenomena in the
Treatment of the Alcoholic," *Pastoral Psychology,* Vol. II
(April, 1951), pp. 28–34.

—— "Crisis and Surrender in Treating Alcoholism," *Quarterly Journal of Studies on Alcohol,* Vol. XXVI (1965), pp. 496–497.

—— "The Ego Factors in Surrender in Alcoholism," *Quarterly Journal of Studies on Alcohol,* Vol. XV (1954), pp. 610–621.

Tyson, Herbert A., "Elements of Religious Experience," *Journal of Religion and Health,* Vol. IV (1965), pp. 441–447.

"Whisky Priests," *Newsweek,* Vol. LXVII (January 10, 1966), p. 58.

Index of Selected Subjects and Authors